MILESTONES
IN
AMERICAN HISTORY
✦✦✦✦✦✦✦✦✦✦✦✦✦✦

THE CUBAN
MISSILE CRISIS
COLD WAR CONFRONTATION

MILESTONES
IN AMERICAN HISTORY

THE ACQUISITION OF FLORIDA

THE ALAMO

ALEXANDER GRAHAM BELL
AND THE TELEPHONE

THE ATTACK ON PEARL HARBOR

THE BOSTON TEA PARTY

THE CALIFORNIA GOLD RUSH

THE CIVIL RIGHTS ACT OF 1964

THE CUBAN MISSILE CRISIS

THE DONNER PARTY

THE ELECTRIC LIGHT

THE EMANCIPATION PROCLAMATION

THE ERIE CANAL

THE GREAT BLACK MIGRATION

THE GREAT DEPRESSION
AND THE NEW DEAL

THE INTERNMENT OF
JAPANESE AMERICANS
DURING WORLD WAR II

THE INVENTION OF
THE MOVING ASSEMBLY LINE

THE LOUISIANA PURCHASE

MANIFEST DESTINY

THE MCCARTHY ERA

THE MONROE DOCTRINE

THE OREGON TRAIL

THE OUTBREAK OF THE CIVIL WAR

THE PONY EXPRESS

THE PROHIBITION ERA

THE RAID ON HARPERS FERRY

THE ROBBER BARONS AND THE
SHERMAN ANTITRUST ACT

THE SALEM WITCH TRIALS

THE SCOPES MONKEY TRIAL

THE SINKING OF THE USS *MAINE*

SPUTNIK/EXPLORER I

THE STOCK MARKET CRASH OF 1929

THE TRANSCONTINENTAL RAILROAD

THE TREATY OF PARIS

THE UNDERGROUND RAILROAD

THE WRIGHT BROTHERS

MILESTONES
IN
AMERICAN HISTORY

THE CUBAN MISSILE CRISIS

COLD WAR CONFRONTATION

HEATHER LEHR WAGNER

CHELSEA HOUSE
An Infobase Learning Company

The Cuban Missile Crisis
Copyright © 2011 by Infobase Learning

Chelsea House
An imprint of Infobase Learning
132 West 31st Street
New York, NY 10001

Library of Congress Cataloging-in-Publication Data

Wagner, Heather Lehr.
The Cuban Missile Crisis : Cold War confrontation / by Heather Lehr Wagner.
  p.   cm. — (Milestones in American history)
Includes bibliographical references and index.
ISBN 978-1-60413-762-0 (hardcover)
1. Cuban Missile Crisis, 1962—Juvenile literature. I. Title. II. Series.

E841.W34 2011
973.922—dc22   2011004460

Chelsea House books are available at special discounts when purchased in bulk quantities for businesses, associations, institutions, or sales promotions. Please call our Special Sales Department in New York at (212) 967-8800 or (800) 322-8755.

You can find Chelsea House on the World Wide Web at http://www.infobaselearning.com

Text design by Erik Lindstrom
Cover design by Alicia Post
Composition by Keith Trego
Cover printed by Yurchak Printing, Landisville, Pa.
Book printed and bound by Yurchak Printing, Landisville, Pa.
Date printed: August 2011
Printed in the United States of America

10 9 8 7 6 5 4 3 2 1

This book is printed on acid-free paper.

All links and Web addresses were checked and verified to be correct at the time of publication. Because of the dynamic nature of the Web, some addresses and links may have changed since publication and may no longer be valid.

CONTENTS

1   The Crisis Begins   1

2   Ghosts of the Past   11

3   Should the United States Attack?   22

4   A Path Is Chosen   34

5   Yes or No   50

6   Conflicting Letters   60

7   Final Attempt   72

8   The Crisis Ends   79

     Chronology   91

     Timeline   92

     Notes   95

     Bibliography   98

     Further Reading   101

     Photo Credits   103

     Index   104

     About the Author   109

The Crisis Begins

The Cuban Missile Crisis began with a knock on the bedroom door of the president of the United States. It was shortly after 8:00 A.M. on Tuesday, October 16, 1962, and President John F. Kennedy was still in bed on the second floor of the White House. Wearing his pajamas and a robe, he was reading the morning newspapers.

Kennedy's national security adviser, McGeorge Bundy, came into the bedroom. He had very bad news for the president. The Central Intelligence Agency (CIA) had evidence that the Soviet Union had installed surface-to-surface nuclear missiles in Cuba, less than 100 miles (161 kilometers) from the United States.

Kennedy's initial reaction was fury. He had just been reading an article on the front page of the *New York Times* in which his predecessor, Dwight D. Eisenhower, had criticized him as "weak on foreign policy."[1] Now Eisenhower's harsh statements seemed to be true, with potentially disastrous consequences for America's national security.

The United States and the Soviet Union had for several years been engaged in escalating tensions in a conflict known as the Cold War. The setting had more recently been in Germany, divided into two separate states after World War II: West Germany (with a democratic form of government) and East Germany (with a Communist dictatorship in place that operated under the influence of the Soviet Union). In Germany's former capital, Berlin, troops from the United States, United Kingdom, France, and the Soviet Union controlled different sectors. But Berlin straddled the two states—East and West Germany—and the Soviet Union ultimately decided to deal with the threat of an armed Western military presence on its border by building a wall separating the eastern and western portions of Berlin in August 1961.

There were other disputes that marked the growing conflict between the United States and the Soviet Union. The United States had recently installed approximately 30 intermediate-range ballistic missiles in Italy and 15 in Turkey as part of NATO (North Atlantic Treaty Organization—a military alliance of democratic countries in Europe and North America) agreements signed in 1959. The Soviet Union viewed these installations as being dangerously close to its borders; the Soviets believed that the missiles could reach their border in approximately 10 minutes.[2]

The Soviet Union had supported the 1959 revolution in Cuba and viewed Cuba's leader, Fidel Castro, as a key ally in the Western Hemisphere. The United States was firmly opposed to the dictatorship of Castro and had made no secret of American efforts to overthrow his regime. In response, Castro had increasingly turned to the Soviets for political and economic support, as well as weapons to prevent an American invasion.

During the summer of 1962, U.S. intelligence had shown that the Soviets were moving numerous weapons into Cuba,

15 OCT 1962
MRBM LAUNCH SITE
SAN DIEGO DE LOS BANOS
22-40N 83-17W

N

PROBABLE
LAUNCHER EQUIPMENT

TENT AREAS

8-MISSILE TRAILERS

EQUIPMENT

CONSTRUCTION

In 1962, U.S. intelligence obtained satellite images that revealed the presence of Soviet missiles in Cuba. This triggered the Cuban Missile Crisis, a tense standoff between the United States and the two Communist countries that almost resulted in war.

including antiaircraft missiles, jet bombers, and cruise missile boats. All these could plausibly be interpreted as defensive weapons, designed to guard Cuba against a potential invasion from the United States. The United States had, through diplomatic channels, learned that no offensive weapons—specifically, no nuclear weapons—would be installed in Cuba. However, the new intelligence reported to Kennedy early on the morning of October 16 made it clear that the Soviet leader, Chairman Nikita S. Khrushchev, had deliberately misled him.

Kennedy scheduled a meeting for that morning to discuss the crisis. This key group of advisers included his brother (Attorney General Robert F. Kennedy), National Security Advisor McGeorge Bundy, Secretary of Defense Robert McNamara, Special Counsel Ted Sorensen, Joint Chiefs of Staff Chairman Maxwell Taylor, Undersecretary of State George Ball, CIA Director John McCone, Secretary of the Treasury Douglas Dillon, and the Soviet specialist at the State Department, Llewellyn Thompson, as well as other intelligence experts. This group was known as ExComm, short for the Executive Committee of the National Security Council.

FIRST REACTIONS

President Kennedy was determined to keep the developments in Cuba secret for as long as possible. For most of the morning, he maintained his previous schedule of appointments, meeting with the family of an astronaut and a Democratic congressman and hosting a conference on mental retardation. Finally, shortly before noon, he and his advisers gathered to discuss the intelligence and how the United States should respond.

Photographs of the Soviet missile installation had been taken by an American U-2 spy plane flying over the western half of Cuba. The plane had taken nearly 1,000 photographs. Now the CIA's chief photo interpreter, Arthur Lundahl, explained to the members of ExComm precisely what the photos revealed.

Initially, the images seemed simply to show slightly grainy shots of Cuban fields, forests, and winding roads. Satellite imaging technology was many years in the future; these photos had been taken when the plane was directly overhead, using a powerful zoom lens.

Lundahl stood next to the president, equipped with a pointer. The images had been labeled; arrows pointed to various spots on the photos, where captions indicated ERECTOR LAUNCHER EQUIPMENT, MISSILE TRAILERS, and TENT AREAS. The sober meeting was briefly interrupted by the arrival of Caroline Kennedy, the president's four-year-old daughter. The president led her out of the room and was gone for a few seconds before returning, and then the grim meeting resumed.

The intelligence showed that the Soviets had installed surface-to-surface nuclear missiles in Cuba. The missiles were less than 100 miles (161 km) from American shores. The CIA's reports indicated that the missiles had a range of 1,174 miles (1,889 km) and could reach much of America's eastern coast. When the missiles were armed and ready to fire, it would take them only 13 minutes to strike and destroy Washington, D.C.

Without the knowledge of most of those gathered, the meeting—like many at the White House—was secretly taped by President Kennedy. The tapes reveal that at no point was there a discussion of simply allowing the missiles to remain in Cuba. The missiles posed a clear and immediate threat to American security. Those at the meeting agreed they must be removed.

Kennedy initially asked how the CIA had determined that the grainy images showed a medium-range ballistic missile. Lundahl explained that the length of the missile provided the necessary clues. The tube shapes identified as missiles in the photographs were determined to be 67 feet (20 meters) long, the same length as missiles displayed at military parades in the Soviet capital of Moscow. Kennedy was informed that the missiles were not yet ready to be fired. Expert analysis suggested that the missiles would need to be fired from a hard surface— packed dirt, concrete, or asphalt.

The key question was timing: How soon would the missiles be ready to fire and launch an attack against the United States? There was no definite answer to this question. The nuclear warheads had not yet been attached to the missiles. Once this took place, the missiles could fire within hours. The CIA experts were unsure precisely whether or not the nuclear warheads had even been moved to the missile sites, but the absence of security at the sites—a guarded storage facility, even a fence—suggested that the nuclear warheads were not yet there.

According to the transcripts, Kennedy asked what advantage the Soviets would derive from setting up the bases.[3] Secretary of State Dean Rusk suggested a connection to the missiles the United States had placed in Turkey, as well as the current tensions in Berlin, noting that there might be a bargaining position between the situation in Berlin and that in Cuba.

The ExComm discussion then focused on the possibility of a quick military strike, designed to take out the missiles before they became operational. This was deemed risky—there was a high likelihood that not all the missiles could be destroyed, opening the United States up to the possibility of a retaliatory strike against American targets with the surviving nuclear weapons. There was a discussion of alerting certain key allies, which Kennedy rejected. "Warning them . . . is warning everybody," he said. "And . . . obviously you can't sort of announce that in four days from now you're going to take them out. They may announce within three days they're going to fire them. Then what'll, what'll we do? Then we don't take 'em out. Of course, we then announce, well if they do that, then we're going to attack with nuclear weapons."[4]

Kennedy stated that there were really three viable options: One was to launch a military strike on the three bases where the missiles were shown to be stored in the photographs. The second option was a broader strike, also targeting airfields, air bases, and anything else thought to be connected to the missiles. The third option involved the broader attack plus a blockade around Cuba.

President John F. Kennedy (*right*) assembled a team of advisers to help him assess the situation in Cuba. Known as the Executive Committee of the National Security Council, or ExComm, this group included members of Kennedy's cabinet, the State Department, and his brother, then-Attorney General Robert F. Kennedy (*left*).

Kennedy's brother, Attorney General Robert Kennedy, offered a fourth option: an invasion of Cuba. He pointed out that without a U.S. invasion of Cuba, the Soviets would simply send in more missiles or target U.S. missile bases in Turkey.

President Kennedy suggested that the group meet again later in the day. He instructed those present to, at a minimum, begin to make the necessary preparations to target the missile bases. The other two options—the broader air strike and the invasion—would be discussed again later in the day.

SECOND MEETING

The president maintained his normal schedule for the afternoon, determined to keep the intelligence—and the possible responses being discussed by ExComm—secret for as long as possible. He hosted a luncheon at the White House in honor of the crown prince of Libya. He gave a speech as planned at a foreign policy conference being held at the State Department for newspaper and television editors. In hindsight, his speech gave a few clues to the grim developments of the past 24 hours. He told reporters that the major challenge facing his presidency was to ensure "the survival of our country . . . without the beginning of the third and perhaps the last war."[5]

At 6:30 P.M., the ExComm members once more gathered in the White House. Marshall Carter, deputy director of the CIA, reported that additional scrutiny of the images showed that there were four missile launchers at each of the three sites, suggesting a capability of 16 to 24 missiles. The missiles, the CIA believed, were solid-propellant, inertial-guidance missiles with a range of 1,100 miles (1,770 km). The estimate was that they could be fully operational within two weeks.

Secretary of State Dean Rusk suggested the possibility of communicating directly with Cuba's leader, Fidel Castro, rather than trying to negotiate with the Soviets. The emphasis would be on clearly indicating to Castro the peril he and his people faced if the missiles were allowed to remain on Cuban soil, hoping to spark a break between Castro and the Soviets. The danger in that approach was that it would signal to the Soviets that the missiles had been spotted and give them an opportunity to move to protect the missiles or quickly prepare them for launch. There was also concern that the Soviets might move against one of the United States' NATO allies.

The CIA signaled its concern regarding the limited-target approach, noting that it would be quite difficult to guarantee that all missiles were hit and destroyed. The first-strike, surprise attack could only be done once and would almost certainly spark some kind of retaliation. Secretary of Defense Robert McNamara stressed this point. "It may well be worth the price," he said. "We must recognize it [a possible military response from the Soviets] by trying to deter it."[6] McNamara noted that this deterrence would involve notifying the Strategic Air Command and putting it on high alert, and at least a partial mobilization of U.S. troops. If the invasion plan was approved, there would need to be a large-scale mobilization of troops, requiring a declaration of a national emergency.

Kennedy believed that, even if the missiles were not ready for launching, even if they were not capable of a successful attack on U.S. soil, there was still a critical need for a firm, strong response. If the Soviet Union was allowed to establish missile bases in Cuba, there was no reason for the Soviets not to set up similar bases in Berlin, Southeast Asia, or any other part of the globe.

Attorney General Robert Kennedy argued for a very aggressive and broad response. If Khrushchev wanted to start a war, he argued, why not "just get into it and get it over with."[7] It was simply a matter of finding a politically acceptable excuse for invading Cuba.

Undersecretary of State George Ball voiced the concern that many in the room were feeling. "What happens beyond that?" he wondered. "You go in there with a surprise attack. You put out all the missiles. This isn't the end. This is the beginning, I think."[8]

The meeting ended with speculation about what precisely might follow. Would a missile attack need to be followed up with an invasion of Cuba? How precisely would American troops occupy the island? Would Castro survive or be overthrown? What would the Soviet response be? Khrushchev would almost certainly retaliate—but where and how? What would the U.S. response then be to that retaliation?

Presidential Counsel Ted Sorensen, who was present at the two meetings, later recalled that while the initial rush of meetings left all involved too busy to be frightened at the enormity of the threat, a time did come when the impact of what was being discussed—the very real possibility of a nuclear war that would target U.S. cities—sank in. "Looking up at the stars," Sorensen wrote in his memoirs, "I thought about those planets or stars that, at some unknown time in ages past, had been extinguished, blinked out, self-destructed. Were we about to join them?"[9]

For 13 days in October 1962, the United States came closer than it ever had before to nuclear war. The events of those 13 days, the actions and decisions made by President John F. Kennedy and Soviet leader Nikita S. Khrushchev and their advisers, reveal the steps that led the world to the brink of nuclear war—a war that would undoubtedly have annihilated vast stretches of the United States and the Soviet Union—and the moment in which these two leaders stepped back from that brink.

Ghosts of the Past

Throughout the 13 days in October that marked the Cuban Missile Crisis, President Kennedy was aware of the tendency for military strategy and decision making to be based on the past—on the events that had marked the previous war the country had fought. His struggle was to fight that tendency, to develop an effective strategy for interpreting Soviet actions and avoiding nuclear war.

But the past did shape the events that led to this crisis. For nearly two decades, the United States and the Soviet Union had sought to build alliances and establish military superiority in various locations around the world. This Cold War—"cold" because it was not a war in the traditional sense, with weapons firing and battles being fought in specific geographic locations—was particularly tragic because it took place between two countries that had been allies. The Soviet Union and the

United States had been part of an alliance during World War II, committed to defeating Nazi Germany. Shortly after Germany was defeated, however, the alliance collapsed as well.

The Soviet Union had suffered heavy losses during World War II. In addition to devastated cities and a heavily damaged infrastructure, some 15 to 20 million of its citizens died during the war. It lost more citizens than any other country in the war; in comparison, the second-highest losses were suffered by Poland, which lost 5.8 million, followed by Germany, which lost 4.5 million.[1]

The legacy of World War II could be measured not only in lives lost, but in economic destruction and in a sense that there was a need to shape new political institutions and alliances to ensure that this kind of devastating war could never happen again. The approach to this postwar reconstruction marked the beginning of the divide between the Soviet Union and the United States. While the Soviet Union faced the daunting task of rebuilding vast stretches of its country and dealing with the crippling loss of manpower, in the United States the mission was one of reconversion rather than reconstruction—converting plants that had built tanks back into plants producing cars, building homes for America's expanding population, and redirecting factories building military aircraft into the new business of producing commercial aircraft.[2]

The end of World War II also marked the end of an era in which foreign policy was dominated by the so-called Great Powers, empires that had governed much of the world. Throughout much of the nineteenth century and well into the first half of the twentieth century, for example, the British and French empires had established colonies and areas of influence in the Middle East, Asia, and Africa. International relations had been based on a Europe-centered system.

Following World War II, these once-great empires no longer had the resources or the infrastructure to police great stretches of the world. Their countries had suffered during the war and now were facing economic hardship as they sought to rebuild. Their citizens were no longer willing to financially support colonies and territories in distant parts of the globe. They wanted to reserve their scarce economic resources for reconstruction efforts in their own cities and towns. Powerful nations like Italy, Japan, and Germany had been defeated and were now occupied.

The result was a power vacuum, one that the United States and the Soviet Union sought to fill in the years immediately following World War II. The former allies were soon arguing over the occupation of Austria, Germany, Italy, Japan, and Korea. Eastern Europe, which had been governed by Nazi administrations during the war, was another source of conflict, as the United States and the Soviet Union each sought to establish a presence there. Each newly independent country presented a new opportunity for conflict, as the two competing powers sought new military bases, markets for exports, and investment opportunities.

The former allies first came into conflict over the division of Europe after World War II. Much of Eastern Europe had been occupied by Soviet troops as they fought their way west to Germany and its capital, Berlin. In conferences held with the Soviet Union, Britain, and the United States after the war, negotiations mapped out "zones of influence" for the allies in Europe and the Far East. The Americans believed that the Soviet Union had agreed to hold free elections in many of these occupied territories—in countries like Bulgaria, Czechoslovakia, Hungary, Poland, and Romania. These countries quickly came under Communist control, however, with governments in power that were firmly allied with the Soviet Union. The divisions between Western Europe and Eastern Europe grew so clear that British leader Winston Churchill described an "iron curtain" that had descended over Europe in 1946.

THE WALL

It was in Berlin that this conflict was clearly illustrated. Postwar treaties stated that the German city (like much of Germany) was to be occupied by four countries—the United States, the Soviet Union, Britain, and France—and governed by military governments until a national government could be reestablished and the country reunified. But Berlin itself was located within the German zone occupied by the Soviet Union.

On June 27, 1948, the Soviet Union imposed a blockade on the western portion of Berlin (East Berlin was controlled by the Soviets). No cars or trains were allowed into the city. The United States responded by launching an air campaign, dropping supplies into the city from airplanes. The blockade was not lifted by the Soviet Union until May 12, 1949. That same year, separate governments were formed for East and West Germany. In the west, a democratic system of government was put in place; in the east, a Communist system continued to govern the people.

From 1945 to 1961, more than 3 million people fled the Soviet Zone and East Berlin, half of them leaving through West Berlin. In 1960 alone, some 360,000 permanently left for the West.[3] On a daily basis, thousands of Germans crossed from one side to another for a variety of reasons. As it became clear that those living in the western part of the city enjoyed a far superior standard of living and greater access to material goods than those living in the east, this became an increasing source of embarrassment and annoyance to the Communist regime in power in the east and its Soviet allies.

Early on the morning of August 13, 1961, some eight months after John F. Kennedy had become president of the United States, temporary barriers were put up at the boundaries separating East and West Berlin. The roads linking the two sections of the city were ripped up. Police stood guard at the barriers, turning away all traffic. Coils of barbed wire were strung along the barrier, stretching some 27 miles (43.5 km), followed

Designed to prevent East Germans from defecting to the democratic enclave in West Berlin, Soviet officials built a wall through the city. Berliners awoke one morning in 1961 to find themselves in a divided city.

over the next few days by a solid stone wall built by East German construction workers, supervised by police and militia. In a very few days, streets and even houses were separated from each other, and the subway lines that had once connected the two sections of Germany were cut. Unlike many barriers, this Berlin Wall was intended to keep people in, not out.

KHRUSHCHEV AND KENNEDY

By 1962, the conflict in Germany had echoed throughout much of the world. It seemed that large sections of the globe were being divided up into separate zones of influence, and the United States and the Soviet Union were symbolically lining up on separate sides of many borders. The two nations were led by very different men. The 45-year-old American president, John F. Kennedy, was the youngest man ever elected president. The former Massachusetts senator, son of a millionaire, was charming and handsome, with a glamorous wife and two young children. Shortly after assuming office, Kennedy had experienced his first serious foreign policy failure, known as The Bay of Pigs Invasion. He had given approval for a band of armed and trained Cuban exiles to invade their homeland in an effort to overthrow the Communist regime of Fidel Castro. The mission had been an embarrassing failure; the exiles had been captured and thrown into prison. Castro, an ally of the Soviet Union, had made public the evidence showing the U.S. involvement in this campaign against his government.

Stopping an expected American invasion of Cuba was one reason why the Soviets had secretly placed the missiles in Cuba. "We didn't want to unleash a war," Soviet leader Khrushchev told colleagues at the time. "We just wanted to frighten them, to restrain the United States in regard to Cuba."[4]

Nikita Khrushchev was 68 years old at the time of the Cuban missile crisis. He had risen up through the Soviet political system from a humble background (he was the son of Ukrainian peasants) because of his ruthlessness, his skill at

Following the death of Joseph Stalin, Nikita Khrushchev (*left*) emerged as the leader of the Soviet Union. A more experienced politician, Khrushchev was unimpressed when he met President Kennedy (*right*) in Vienna, Austria, in 1961.

pleasing his predecessor Joseph Stalin, and his talent for the patience and strength needed to survive in the Soviet bureaucracy. He was some 23 years older than Kennedy and had not been impressed by the American president when he met him in Vienna, Austria.

Khrushchev had enjoyed two political coups—the Soviet Union was the first nation to launch a man into space and had tested the world's largest nuclear bomb. Yet he was acutely aware of the Soviet Union's vulnerability. The United States still enjoyed military superiority, and with U.S. military bases ringing the Soviet Union, including military installations in Turkey

(*continues on page 20*)

JOHN F. KENNEDY

The thirty-fifth president of the United States, John Fitzgerald Kennedy, became president in 1961 at the age of 43, making him the youngest man ever elected to the presidency and the first Catholic. He was born into a wealthy, politically connected Boston family. While a student at Harvard, he wrote a best-selling book titled *Why England Slept*, published in 1940, which examined the conditions in England in the 1930s prior to World War II (his father, Joseph Kennedy, had been appointed ambassador to England in 1938).

After Kennedy graduated from Harvard, he enlisted in the U.S. Navy. Kennedy served in the South Pacific during World War II as commander of a small, motor torpedo boat, or PT boat. In August 1943, his boat was rammed by a Japanese destroyer and sank; Kennedy and his crew survived. His older brother, Joseph Jr., was killed in the war while flying a bombing mission over Europe. Their father had hoped that Joseph would one day be president; after his death, the father turned to John as the son who would become president.

In 1946, at the age of 29, John Kennedy was elected to the U.S. Congress. He served three terms, then ran for and was successfully elected to the U.S. Senate in 1952. In 1953, he married Jacqueline Bouvier; the two had three children, one of whom (a son, Patrick, born while Kennedy was president) died in infancy.

Throughout his life, Kennedy battled various illnesses. Sickly as a child, he contracted malaria while serving in the Pacific and also suffered from Addison's disease. In 1956, Kennedy's *Profiles in Courage* was published. The book—written while Kennedy was recovering from back surgery—profiled Americans who had taken

unpopular but moral stands during challenging circumstances; it won the Pulitzer Prize for biography in 1957.

In 1956, Kennedy made an unsuccessful effort to gain the vice presidential slot on the Democratic ticket. The Democratic nominee, Adlai Stevenson, instead chose Estes Kefauver; the ticket was firmly defeated by the Republican ticket of Dwight Eisenhower and Richard Nixon. In 1960, Kennedy won the Democratic nomination for president, and in a close election defeated Richard Nixon. One of the highlights of the campaign was a series of televised debates, which proved very successful for the attractive, telegenic Kennedy.

Kennedy faced several domestic challenges during his presidency, including an economic recession and the growing activism that marked the civil rights struggle in the 1960s. In addition to handling crises in Cuba and Berlin, Kennedy was a significant supporter of the U.S. space program, setting a goal for the United States to place a man on the moon by the end of the decade (a goal that was achieved in 1969), and as president he created the Peace Corps.

While Kennedy was in office, the conflict in Vietnam was growing. During his presidency, the number of U.S. military advisers sent to Vietnam increased significantly, and many of his foreign policy advisers would go on to become architects of the disastrous U.S. efforts in Southeast Asia.

On November 22, 1963, while traveling through Dallas on a campaign trip, President Kennedy was assassinated. His killer, Lee Harvey Oswald, was a former Marine who had defected to the Soviet Union and spent time in Cuba before returning to the United States. Two days after his arrest, Oswald was assassinated by a Dallas nightclub owner, Jack Ruby.

(continued from page 17)
and Japan, there were far more U.S. nuclear missiles targeting the Soviet Union than there were Soviet nuclear missiles targeting the United States.

Khrushchev decided to use Cuba as a base for Soviet nuclear ballistic missiles. "The Americans had surrounded our country with military bases and threatened us with nuclear weapons," he later recalled, "and now they would learn just what it feels like to have enemy missiles pointing at you; we'd be doing nothing more than giving them a little of their own medicine."[5] His plan was to transport the missiles secretly to Cuba, revealing them only after they were fully in place and ready for use if needed. They would be sent by ship, which was considered safer than transport by airplane (if the planes crashed, a nuclear explosion might result).

By late August 1962, the Kennedy administration was aware that a major supply effort was under way, as large Soviet tankers churned across the Atlantic toward Cuba. Many of Kennedy's advisers believed that the Soviets were arming their ally with conventional weapons, as they had done for several other allies. However, a few in the administration, including the president's brother, Attorney General Robert Kennedy, believed that the shipments might contain nuclear missiles.

A meeting was scheduled between Robert Kennedy and the Soviet ambassador, Anatoly Dobrynin, on September 4, 1962. The meeting had been requested by the Soviets. At that meeting, Kennedy clearly stated that the increase in Soviet military supplies and specialists being shipped to Cuba was a cause of great concern to the U.S. government. The attorney general then noted that rockets with "small nuclear charges" might be included in the shipments. Dobrynin, who had not been included in the details of Khrushchev's plan to place nuclear weapons in Cuba, firmly replied that "the Soviet Union supports the nontransfer and the nonproliferation of nuclear weapons,"[6] offering to have this position clarified if necessary.

After this meeting, President Kennedy issued a statement containing a warning. "There is no evidence of any organized combat force in Cuba from any Soviet bloc country; of military bases provided to Russia ... of the presence of offensive ground-to-ground missiles; or of other significant offensive capability in either Cuban hands or under Soviet direction and guidance. Were it to be otherwise, the gravest issues would arise."[7]

By late September, Soviet cargo ships with specially designed holds had transported numerous medium-range ballistic missiles to Cuba. These were the R-12 (also known as SS-4) medium-range ballistic missiles. They were 74 feet (22.6 m) long, and one missile was the equivalent of one million tons (907,185 metric tons) of TNT (in comparison, Hiroshima was destroyed by an explosion equivalent to 14,000 tons [12,700 mt] of TNT).[8] They had a 14,000-mile (22,531-km) range and could reach points as far west as El Paso, Texas, and as far east as Washington, D.C. On October 16, the president learned that nuclear missiles had been placed in Cuba.

Should the United States Attack?

For the next several days, President Kennedy continued to follow his planned public activities while members of ExComm met and debated possible responses to the Soviet missiles in Cuba. On October 17, 1962, the day after the president first learned of the missiles, six U-2 missions were ordered over the skies of Cuba, the spy planes flying along the length of the island, snapping photographs and trying to determine the status of the known missiles and discover whether there were any additional missile sites. The question of which allies would be notified and when was also debated, but the largest focus was whether or not there should be a military response and if yes, what form that would take.

Initially, many members of ExComm—including the president's brother, Robert Kennedy—felt that the United States should target the missile sites in a bombing raid. The problem

ROBERT F. KENNEDY

Robert Francis Kennedy was born in 1925, the seventh of nine children in the wealthy, politically connected Kennedy family. He served in the U.S. Navy during World War II, and then graduated from Harvard in 1948 and received a law degree from the University of Virginia three years later.

In 1950, he married Ethel Skakel; the couple eventually had 11 children. He managed his older brother John's successful campaign for the U.S. Senate in 1952, and then served briefly on the Senate Subcommittee on Investigations chaired by Senator Joseph McCarthy. Disturbed by McCarthy's controversial methods and allegations that traitors were shaping U.S. foreign policy, Kennedy ultimately resigned from the subcommittee. He later worked as chief counsel for a Senate committee investigating corruption in trade unions.

Robert Kennedy served as the campaign manager for his brother John's successful campaign for the presidency in 1960. He was then appointed attorney general, becoming one of his brother's closest advisers during the Kennedy presidency.

Shortly after John F. Kennedy's assassination, Robert Kennedy resigned as attorney general. In 1964, he ran a successful campaign for the U.S. Senate seat in New York. As a senator, he focused much of his energy on the needs of the poor and underprivileged children. Later, he became a critic of the increasing involvement of the United States in Vietnam, taking responsibility for his own role in advancing the war while his brother was president.

In 1968, he ran his own campaign for the presidency, focusing on civil rights issues, poverty, and the war in Vietnam. His campaign was cut short when he was assassinated on June 5, 1968, in Los Angeles, only hours after winning California's important Democratic primary. He died the next day, at the age of 42.

was that the military could not guarantee that all missiles would be destroyed in a bombing, leaving open the possibility that the surviving missiles (and any others in sites not discovered by the United States) might then be launched against the United States. It was Robert Kennedy who gradually emerged as the group's leader in the absence of the president. Enjoying a special security as the president's brother, he was able to speak freely without worrying about politics or fearing for his job, challenging assumptions and debating each suggestion. His presence also added a certain moderation to the discussions, as group members knew that anything said in his presence might well be reported back to the president. The group would meet almost continuously for the next 12 days. The group would frequently change their positions, swayed by debate, new evidence, and changing events as the impact of each decision was realized and the threat of nuclear war grew more likely.

"And so we argued, and so we disagreed," Robert Kennedy later wrote in his memoir of the crisis, *Thirteen Days*, "all dedicated, intelligent men, disagreeing and fighting about the future of their country, and of mankind. Meanwhile, time was slowly running out."[1]

The team felt strongly that the president should continue his regular schedule of appearances and activities until a firm course of action had been decided and approved. They also debated notifying leaders in the Senate and House of Representatives but decided that this, too, should be postponed until the president had firmly determined what action would be taken, to avoid any leaks to the media or public.

As a result, that day—as the prospect of nuclear war was debated—President Kennedy found himself flying to Connecticut for a political rally in support of Democratic candidate Abraham Ribicoff, who was running for the Senate to succeed the retiring Republican senator Prescott Bush (father of future president George H.W. Bush and grandfather of future president George W. Bush). The president gave little hint of the crisis, encouraging those at the rally to ensure the election of the Democratic candidate.

THREE OPTIONS

Gradually, the members of ExComm narrowed the options for a possible response to three recommendations for the president's consideration. The first was political action—diplomatic pressure and a warning to the Soviets—followed by a military strike (an attack against the missile sites) if a satisfactory response was not received within a set time frame. The second was an immediate military strike, without advance warning. The third response was political action—diplomatic pressure and a warning—followed by a total naval blockade, in which a fleet of U.S. ships would surround Cuba and prevent any Soviet ships from entering Cuban waters and delivering additional military supplies or equipment.

The proposals for political action included letters to Chairman Khrushchev warning him that the missile bases would be attacked if the missiles were not immediately removed, requests for a meeting between Khrushchev and Kennedy, letters to the Cuban leader Fidel Castro warning of the consequences of the missiles' continued presence on his island, action involving the United Nations (UN), and other diplomatic proposals.

At the beginning, during that first meeting on October 16, nearly all members of ExComm favored the second response— an immediate air strike against the nuclear missile sites before they could become operational. Presidential adviser Ted Sorensen, a member of ExComm, described the group's hope that "U.S. bombers could swoop in, eliminate the sites, and fly away, leaving the problem swiftly, magically ended."[2] But the U.S. Air Force could only guarantee the destruction of 60 percent of the missiles and insisted that it would first need to bomb all Soviet surface-to-air missile sites, all Cuban antiaircraft sites, and all Soviet and Cuban airfields, effectively eliminating any threat to U.S. aircraft and preventing planes and bombers from targeting U.S. soil. This option would result in bombing a significant portion of Cuban territory. There was also discussion of the possibility of invading and occupying Cuba after an attack.

The ExComm members invited former secretary of state Dean Acheson to join them as a consultant. Acheson had served as secretary of state from 1949 to 1953, during President Harry Truman's second term. When asked for his advice in this early meeting, Acheson replied that he supported the option to bomb the missile sites in Cuba. Acheson was then asked what he thought the Soviet response would be to such an attack. He replied that they would probably bomb U.S. missile sites in Turkey. He then said that the United States would be obligated to bomb Soviet missile sites inside Russia. When pressed for what the Soviet response would be to that attack, Acheson paused and finally replied, "By then, we hope cooler heads will prevail."[3]

There was little initial support for the third option—the option of using a naval blockade. One of the few supporters of this option was Secretary of Defense Robert McNamara. McNamara felt that this option offered pressure on the Soviets, but a limited pressure that could be increased if necessary. It was pressure that made clear the United States' unwillingness to accept the continued presence of the Soviet missiles in Cuba. It was pressure that the United States could control. McNamara felt that the air strike was a far more dangerous and uncertain option, an option that might ultimately have to be used but that should not be the first choice.

Those opposed to the blockade argued that it was too little, too late—it did not remove the missiles, since the missiles were already in Cuba, and did not prevent work from continuing at the missile sites to make the missiles operational. They also feared that installing a military blockade around Cuba might prompt the Soviets to do the same in Berlin. If the United

The majority of ExComm members initially believed the United States should bomb the Soviet missile sites in Cuba. Secretary of Defense Robert McNamara (*above*), however, proposed a naval blockade—an option that gave the United States more control in the situation.

States stated that the missiles needed to be removed from Cuba before the blockade could be lifted, the Soviets might make a similar demand for the removal of missiles around the Soviet Union.

There were many unanswered questions when the October 16 meeting finally disbanded. Would the Soviets attack Berlin or U.S. missile sites in Turkey? What would prevent Soviet or Cuban military officers from firing the missiles against the United States? What would happen if only a portion of the missiles were destroyed in an air attack?

MORE MISSILES, GREATER THREAT

Wednesday's U-2 flights produced alarming photographs that proved that there were additional missile sites in Cuba. These additional installations had at least 16 and as many as 32 missiles, each with a range of more than 1,000 miles (1,609 km). Military experts studied the photographs and reported that the missiles could be in operation within one week. The photos showed that the missiles were being directed at certain American cities. CIA estimates suggested that, within a few minutes of those missiles being fired, 80 million Americans would be dead.

On the morning of Thursday, October 18—the third day of the Cuban Missile Crisis—President Kennedy asked the members of ExComm to join him in the Cabinet Room. They then gave the president their recommendations, laying out the options.

The Joint Chiefs of Staff (America's military leaders) favored immediate military action. The air force chief of staff, General Curtis LeMay, was particularly outspoken, arguing with the president that an air strike was essential. When the president asked what the Russian response would be, LeMay firmly stated that there would be no response from the Soviets.

Former secretary of state Dean Acheson also strongly supported an air strike. For Acheson, it was a security issue—the president of the United States was responsible for ensuring the security of Americans. The missiles threatened that security and must be destroyed.

Others, including Secretary of Defense McNamara and Robert Kennedy, outlined their support for a naval blockade. A debate began about whether or not the Soviet ships would turn back or permit U.S. officials to inspect the cargo on their ships.

Yet another issue needed to be considered: Some favored sending an immediate letter to Khrushchev, and then deciding whether or not to follow with an air strike or blockade. Those who favored sending the letter felt that this would alert

Khrushchev to the U.S. discovery of the missiles and give him time to formulate his response, to avoid allowing military officials based in Cuba to swiftly give the order to fire the missiles without waiting for the approval of the Soviet leader.

The letter was also a response to concerns about public opinion, should the United States without warning begin a bombing campaign against a third world country (Cuba). Robert Kennedy expressed his worry that the perception would be of a surprise attack by a very large nation against a very small one. "Our struggle against Communism throughout the world was far more than physical survival," Robert Kennedy later wrote. "It had as its essence our heritage and our ideals, and these we must not destroy."[4] The attorney general recalled this moral question as being the focus of much debate during the first five days of the crisis, with more time being spent on this than any other single matter. There were proposals for a letter to be sent to Khrushchev or to Castro 24 hours before an air strike, or for leaflets and pamphlets to be dropped over Cuba before the attack, listing the targets to give the population time to evacuate those locations. "We struggled and fought with one another and with our consciences," Robert Kennedy wrote in his memoirs of that time, "for it was a question that deeply troubled us all."[5]

Ted Sorensen was asked to draft a warning letter from President Kennedy to Chairman Khrushchev, in case this option should ultimately be selected. There were many requirements, as Sorensen noted: "It must withstand the scrutiny of the American people, foreign diplomats, and posterity. It could not read like an ultimatum, because a superpower would not yield to an ultimatum. It should not be complicated, because Khrushchev would tie us up in negotiations for weeks while the missile sites were completed. It should not be so soft that he would think he could get away with it, or so hard that the world would blame us for a nuclear holocaust. It must not provoke Khrushchev into notifying his forces that the missiles had been discovered and should be immediately fired, thereby launching World War III."[6]

It is perhaps not surprising that Sorensen found this to be an impossible task. When he finally reported back to the ExComm members that he could not produce a draft letter that would meet all of their requirements, support for the air strike option began to fade.

In an ironic twist, a meeting had been previously scheduled that same day with Soviet foreign minister Andrei Gromyko. The meeting had been scheduled long before the discovery of the missiles; now President Kennedy had to decide whether or not to confront the Soviets' chief diplomat with what the United States had learned. Finally, not yet having decided what course of action he was going to take, he decided to continue with the meeting and simply listen to what Gromyko had to say.

At 5:00 P.M., Gromyko and his interpreter were ushered into the Oval Office. Gromyko began the conversation by discussing Berlin. The Soviet position was that Western troops should be removed from Berlin to make it a "free city." Kennedy calmly responded that the U.S. position was that Western troops were necessary to ensure the city's freedom and survival. Gromyko then noted that Khrushchev planned to come to the United States in late November to address the UN General Assembly, and perhaps a meeting between the two leaders might be useful. Kennedy replied that he would be happy to meet with Khrushchev but could not bargain about Berlin, since other nations had an interest in the city.

Gromyko then said that he wished to raise the issue of Cuba. The president wondered if he would mention the existence of the missiles, but he did not. Instead, he complained of what he described as "anti-Cuba" actions by the United States. Cuba was a "baby facing a giant," in Gromyko's words. It was not a threat to anyone. The president, Gromyko continued, appreciated frankness, so he would be frank. This was not the nineteenth century, "when the world was divided up into

Conducting air strikes on Cuba would likely cause the Soviets to launch missiles against U.S. forces in other parts of the world. Above, red rockets move into Red Square during a Moscow parade celebrating the anniversary of the Bolshevik Revolution.

colonies and . . . the victims of aggression could only be heard weeks after any attack."[7] Khrushchev had instructed him to make it clear, Gromyko continued, that Soviet aid to Cuba was "solely for the purpose of contributing to defense capabilities of Cuba. . . . If it were otherwise, the Soviet government would never become involved in rendering such assistance."[8]

President Kennedy, seated in a rocking chair next to Gromyko, replied that there should be no misunderstanding of the position of the United States, a position that had been made clear in meetings between Attorney General Robert Kennedy and Soviet ambassador Anatoly Dobrynin and in the president's own public statements. To further cement this, Kennedy read aloud from a statement he had made on September 4, which pointed out the serious consequences that would follow if the Soviet Union placed missiles or offensive weapons in Cuba. Gromyko assured him that this would never happen.

The president then reminded Gromyko of what he had told Khrushchev when the two leaders had met in Vienna, Austria: The United States and the Soviet Union were large countries. History would judge their competition. Neither of them should "take actions leading to a confrontation of our two countries."[9] The Soviet foreign minister assured him that the United States had no reason for concern.

As Gromyko and Kennedy were concluding their meeting, the members of ExComm were meeting at the State Department. Concerned about preserving secrecy, the group was not meeting at the White House. The president had also ordered the group's members not to draw attention to themselves by traveling in large fleets of cars. So it was that at 10:00 P.M. that Thursday, some of the leading members of President Kennedy's administration piled into a single limousine, some even sitting on each other's laps, and entered the White House in an underground garage to give the president their latest recommendations.

In their meeting at the State Department, the group had gradually come to favor the naval blockade option—which they were now calling a "quarantine," as a naval blockade would require an official declaration of war by the United States. The quarantine offered the ability to select any of the other options, if necessary, and the vote at the State Department had been 11 to 6, with 11 in favor of the naval quarantine and 6 favoring the air strike.

Robert Kennedy noted in his memoirs that the meeting began in an orderly way, with the group presenting their conclusions to the president. "However, as people talked, as the President raised probing questions, minds and opinions began to change again, and not only on small points. For some, it was from one extreme to another—supporting an air attack at the beginning of the meeting and, by the time we left the White House, supporting no action at all."[10]

President Kennedy was clearly frustrated. He still did not know what action to pursue, nor apparently did his advisers, some of whom were now suggesting that perhaps no response at all was required. He ordered the ExComm members to go back and try to reach agreement on their recommendation. He asked Ted Sorensen to prepare two different speeches that he could deliver to the American public on Monday night—one if he chose to order an air attack, the other if he chose to order the naval blockade.

A Path Is Chosen

On Friday, October 19, President Kennedy left Washington for a previously scheduled campaign trip to Chicago. It was becoming increasingly difficult for him to maintain his schedule and give no hint of the critical discussions that were revolving around the very real threat of nuclear war. He was also frustrated by the seeming inability of his advisers to reach a consensus on what course of action the United States should follow. Shortly before his departure, he instructed his brother to urge the members of ExComm to reach a conclusion at once, so that, if it met with his approval, he could broadcast it to the nation that Sunday night.

It was also becoming increasingly difficult for the president to preserve secrecy about the discussions at the highest levels of his administration. Already, reporters for the *Chicago Sun-Times*, the *New York Times*, and the *Miami Herald* were asking

White House Press Secretary Pierre Salinger (who had not
been included in the ExComm discussions) about rumors of
planned U.S. military action against Cuba.

Finally, on the morning of Saturday, October 20, Robert
Kennedy phoned his brother in Chicago and told him that the
members of ExComm were prepared to meet with him. Their
positions were firm, but they were now individually committed
to their decisions and there would be no more switching positions during the course of a discussion. They wanted to present
their final arguments to the president, the arguments in favor
of a naval blockade or an air attack. Only one person—the
president—could make the final decision on which course the
United States would ultimately pursue.

Press Secretary Salinger announced to the media that the
president was suffering from a cold and would immediately
return to Washington. Shortly after 1:30 P.M. that Saturday,
President Kennedy was back at the White House, and that afternoon the president met with members of his National Security
Council, a larger group that included some who had not par-
ticipated in the ExComm discussions.

Multiple options were presented at that meeting for the
president's consideration. Robert Kennedy, in his memoirs,
noted that one member of the Joint Chiefs of Staff suggested
that the president order the use of nuclear weapons, since the
Soviets would undoubtedly use theirs against the United States
in the escalating conflict. "I thought, as I listened," Robert
Kennedy later wrote, "of the many times that I had heard the
military take positions which, if wrong, had the advantage that
no one would be around at the end to know."[1]

The CIA had presented evidence to the president that it
believed at least four of the medium-range ballistic missile sites
were operational. Should the Soviet Union decide to attack,
those missiles could probably be fired within eight hours.

The president was faced with several considerations. One
was the possibility that, if the Soviets learned that the United

States had discovered the existence of the missiles, they might order an immediate nuclear attack on the assumption that the United States was about to go to war. Another was the likelihood that, no matter which response the United States took, the Soviets would retaliate somewhere—if not in Cuba, then most likely in Berlin. Particularly if the United States ordered an air strike against the missiles in Cuba—an air strike that would undoubtedly kill many Soviet soldiers and Cuban allies stationed at the missile sites—the Soviets would be unlikely to accept an attack against their military. This too could quickly escalate into a larger war.

After several days of meetings and debates, ExComm presented the president with two options: an air strike or a naval blockade. There were advantages and disadvantages for each option. An air strike would clearly demonstrate the United States' unwillingness to accept nuclear weapons in Cuba and would also quickly reduce the immediate threat. But military experts had confirmed that they were unable to guarantee that all missiles would be destroyed, and the hundreds of flights necessary for the air strike might lead to massive chaos in Cuba. An invasion might then be necessary.

A naval blockade seemed a better way to avert war. Soviet ships would be prevented from coming within a specified distance of Cuba. Any ships attempting to cross this line would be boarded and their cargo inspected. This option offered an opportunity for negotiations; however, it also would give the Soviets time to delay while they completed work on the missile sites. It also might lead to a military confrontation between the U.S. and Soviet navies.

The president considered his options that night and called for a final meeting of the members of ExComm over breakfast Sunday morning. A poll was taken: Nine members favored an air strike; seven supported the naval blockade, or quarantine. The president attended Mass, then met with General Walter Sweeney, the tactical air chief who would command the air strike on Cuba, if that was the option the president selected. He asked the general to be specific about the percentage of missiles that he could guarantee to destroy. The answer: 90 percent of the known missiles. It was not known how many additional missiles were hidden in Cuba.

This information cemented the president's decision. He would go with the naval quarantine first.

A COURSE OF ACTION

The president's decision was the result of six days of deliberation and discussion with a team of 12 experts assembled to focus specifically on the situation in Cuba. It is important to remember that President Kennedy, when he first learned of the missiles, had initially favored an air strike and, had he made a hasty decision about the American response, might have ordered an air attack on the missile sites.

Author Michael Beschloss notes that contemporary presidents do not have the luxury of those six days; were the Cuban Missile Crisis to have occurred today, "an American television network with access to a private satellite might well have discovered the missiles and announced them to the world only hours after the President had learned about them."[2] Allied leaders might then put pressure on the president not to respond, since similar missiles threatened Western Europe without those nations responding. Political opponents might publicly call on the president to immediately order an air attack and invasion. In the public outcry and debate, it might have been difficult for the president to choose the more moderate option of the naval quarantine.[3]

Presidential adviser Ted Sorensen has expressed his certainty that, had the president selected the air strike option, it would have produced a nuclear war. "Such an air strike and invasion, we have learned, would have brought in response an immediate nuclear assault upon our forces by Soviet troops in Cuba, equipped with tactical nuclear weapons and authorized to use them on their own initiative, thereby precipitating the world's first nuclear exchange, initially limited perhaps to the tactical weapons level, but inevitably and rapidly escalating to an all-out strategic exchange, very possibly lasting until little remained in either country other than radioactive ash. A 'nuclear winter,' I was later told by scientists, might have made this planet uninhabitable for thousands of years."[4]

The president learned that Sunday evening that reporters from the *New York Times* and the *Washington Post* had compiled much of the facts of the crisis and were preparing stories for press. President Kennedy phoned the publishers of the two newspapers and asked them to hold off on their stories for 24 hours; they agreed.

On Monday, October 22, an order was given to evacuate all civilians from the United States' Guantanamo Bay Naval Base in Cuba. Marines began escorting more than 2,000 women and children to planes and ships for the evacuation. At the same time, messages were sent to any congressional leaders who were vacationing, asking them to return at once to Washington. Democratic congressional leader Hale Boggs of Louisiana was fishing in the Gulf of Mexico when a military helicopter appeared overhead and dropped a bottle into the water next to his boat. The bottle contained a note: "Call Operator 18, Washington. Urgent message from the President."[5] In a short time, Boggs and the other congressional leaders were on board air force jets flying swiftly back to Washington.

At 4:00 P.M., all members of the president's cabinet assembled at the White House. The president told them that he had decided to order a naval blockade of Cuba in response to the Soviet deployment of missiles there. Certain key allies—England, Germany, and France—were informed of the decision in advance by representatives sent by the president. Former secretary of state Dean Acheson was sent to meet with French president Charles de Gaulle in Paris. In those days before secure phone lines and supersonic jets, Acheson flew all night from Washington to Paris in order to meet with de

As Kennedy debated the three options ExComm presented to him, he met with Soviet foreign minister Andrei Gromyko (*center*). The meeting revealed nothing to Kennedy, and both Gromyko and Soviet ambassador Anatoly Dobrynin (*left*) seemed genuinely shocked when they were later told about the missiles in Cuba.

Gaulle. Acheson offered to show him the photographs proving the presence of Soviet missiles in Cuba, but de Gaulle replied that it was not necessary. "A great nation like yours would not act if there were any doubt about the evidence,"[6] he said.

Two hours before the president was scheduled to give a televised address to the nation, he met with 17 leaders of Congress and informed them of the situation and his decision. Many of them, including fellow Democrats, openly disagreed with his choice of the naval blockade, arguing that an air strike and invasion were the only sensible responses. Kennedy reassured them that he had considered his decision for several days, and that his hope was that the crisis could be resolved without a devastating war. A nuclear war might result in the deaths of millions of

THE WILL AND DETERMINATION OF THE UNITED STATES

On October 22, 1962, the Soviet ambassador to the United States was given a letter from President Kennedy to Chairman Khrushchev. The letter confirmed that the United States was now aware of the presence of Soviet missiles in Cuba and warned Khrushchev that the United States would do "whatever must be done to protect its own security," as noted in this excerpt:

DEAR MR. CHAIRMAN: A copy of the statement I am making tonight concerning developments in Cuba and the reaction of my Government thereto has been handed to your Ambassador in Washington. In view of the gravity of the developments to which I refer, I want you to know immediately and accurately the position of my government in this matter.

In our discussions and exchanges on Berlin and other international questions, the one thing that has most concerned me has been the possibility that your Government would not correctly understand the will and determination of the United States in any given situation, since I have not assumed that you or any other sane man would, in this nuclear age, deliberately plunge the world into war which it is crystal clear no country could win and which could only result in catastrophic consequences to the whole world, including the aggressor.

At our meeting in Vienna and subsequently, I expressed our readiness and desire to find, through peaceful negotiation, a solution

Americans; he did not want to chance this until all other possibilities had been explored. He then returned to prepare for his televised speech to the nation.

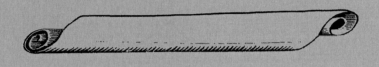

to any and all problems that divide us. At the same time, I made clear that in view of the objectives of the ideology to which you adhere, the United States could not tolerate any action on your part which in a major way disturbed the existing over-all balance of power in the world. . . .

It was in order to avoid any incorrect assessment on the part of your Government with respect to Cuba that I publicly stated that if certain developments in Cuba took place, the United States would do whatever must be done to protect its own security and that of its allies. . . .

Despite this, the rapid development of long-range missile bases and other offensive weapons systems in Cuba has proceeded. I must tell you that the United States is determined that this threat to the security of this hemisphere be removed. At the same time, I wish to point out that the action we are taking is the minimum necessary to remove the threat to the security of the nations of this hemisphere. The fact of this minimum response should not be taken as a basis, however, for any misjudgment on your part.

I hope that your Government will refrain from any action which would widen or deepen this already grave crisis and that we can agree to resume the path of peaceful negotiations.

Thomas Fensch, ed., "Letter from President Kennedy to Chairman Khrushchev, October 22, 1962," in *The Kennedy-Khrushchev Letters.* The Woodlands, Tex.: New Century Books, 2001, pp. 298–230.

At approximately 6:00 P.M., one hour before the president's speech, Secretary of State Dean Rusk met with the Soviet ambassador to the United States, Anatoly Dobrynin. Dobrynin had not been informed by his government of the presence of the missiles in Cuba. Now he not only learned of the missiles but was handed a copy of President Kennedy's speech and given a private letter for Khrushchev, warning him not to underestimate American "will and determination."[7] Secretary of State Rusk thought that Dobrynin seemed to "age 10 years" during the course of their brief meeting; reporters noted that he was "ashen-faced and visibly shaken" when he left. When the reporters called out their questions, asking if a crisis was about to erupt, Dobrynin replied, "What do you think?"[8] and waved a copy of the envelope Rusk had handed to him, then hurried to his limousine.

THE PUBLIC IS INFORMED

At 7:00 P.M. on October 22, President Kennedy addressed the nation. Ted Sorensen described it as "not the best speech of JFK's presidency, but it surely was his most important. It fully informed the American people and the world of what appeared to be the greatest danger to our country in history, without creating national panic, despair, or a cry for either surrender or war."[9]

"Good evening, my fellow citizens," President Kennedy began. "This Government, as promised, has maintained the closest surveillance of the Soviet military buildup on the island of Cuba. Within the past weeks, unmistakable evidence has established the fact that a series of offensive missile sites is now in preparation on that imprisoned island." These missiles, Kennedy explained, had "nuclear strike capability against the Western Hemisphere."[10]

The president continued, explaining that the missiles included medium-range ballistic missiles capable of striking Washington, D.C., the Panama Canal, Mexico City, or any city

On October 22, 1962, President Kennedy addressed the nation in a television and radio broadcast explaining the events of the past two weeks. More than 100 million Americans listened as Kennedy announced the discovery of the missiles, how the United States would respond, and the possible repercussions if the situation escalated into war.

in the southeastern part of the United States. He added that other sites were being constructed for intermediate-range ballistic missiles that were capable of striking most of the major cities in the Western Hemisphere, as far north as Canada and as far south as Peru. Kennedy said:

> Neither the United States of America nor the world community of nations can tolerate deliberate deception and

offensive threats on the part of any nation, large or small. We no longer live in a world where only the actual firing of weapons represents a sufficient challenge to a nation's security to constitute maximum peril. Nuclear weapons are so destructive and ballistic missiles are so swift that any substantially increased possibility of their use or any sudden change in their deployment may well be regarded as a definite threat to peace. . . . Our policy has been one of patience and restraint, as befits a peaceful and powerful nation, which leads a world-wide alliance. We have been determined not to be diverted from our central concerns by mere irritants and fanatics. But now further action is required—and it is underway; and these actions may only be the beginning. We will not prematurely or unnecessarily risk the costs of world-wide nuclear war in which even the fruits of victory would be ashes in our mouth—but neither will we shrink from that risk at any time it must be faced.[11]

Next, the president discussed the initial steps he had ordered. First, a quarantine would be initiated against all offensive military equipment being shipped to Cuba. All ships destined for Cuba, if found to contain offensive weapons in their cargoes, would be turned back.

Second, the United States would continue and, in fact, increase its close surveillance of Cuba and the military buildup occurring on the island. Should this buildup continue, the president warned, further action would be considered justified, and he had instructed the U.S. military to prepare for any eventualities.

Third, the president stated that it would be the policy of the United States to view any nuclear missile launched from Cuba against any nation in the Western Hemisphere as an attack by the Soviet Union on the United States, requiring full retaliation upon the Soviet Union.

The president continued, explaining that he had ordered the reinforcement of the U.S. military base at Guantanamo, the evacuation of dependents and civilians there, and the placement of additional military units on standby alert. He called for an emergency meeting of the Security Council of the United Nations to take action against the Soviet Union. The United States, he stated, would call for a resolution specifying that the Soviet Union must promptly dismantle and withdraw all offensive weapons from Cuba under the supervision of UN inspectors before the quarantine would be lifted.

The president concluded by calling upon Khrushchev to "halt and eliminate this clandestine, reckless, and provocative threat to world peace." Kennedy continued: "My fellow citizens, let no one doubt that this is a difficult and dangerous effort on which we have set out. No one can foresee precisely what course it will take or what costs or casualties will be incurred. Many months of sacrifice and self-discipline lie ahead— months in which both our patience and our will will be tested, months in which many threats and denunciations will keep us aware of our dangers. But the greatest danger of all would be to do nothing."[12]

The television address lasted slightly more than 15 minutes. Ted Sorensen, who wrote the speech, notes that the president decided not to show pictures on television of the types of missiles that were being built, nor the grainy pictures of the missile sites, out of concern that it might lead to panic. "We wanted to reassure Americans and the world that the president knew what was happening, that the missiles would not be permitted to stay, and that a prudent, limited response had been formulated and was ready to be implemented,"[13] Sorensen explained. Nonetheless, historian Michael Beschloss described the address as "probably the most alarming ever delivered by an American President."[14] More than 100 million Americans watched the speech; it was the largest audience for a presidential address up until that time.[15]

WAITING FOR A RESPONSE

That night, after giving the speech, the president had no idea what the Soviet response would be. Would there be an air attack? An action against a U.S. post or ally elsewhere in the world? There was concern and uncertainty when he retired for the night, and some slight relief the next morning as he woke to learn that the Soviets had not attacked NATO missiles in Turkey, nor launched a blockade in Berlin. By the time members of ExComm gathered with the president at 10:00 A.M. on Tuesday, October 23, Robert Kennedy writes that there was a slight feeling of relaxation among the group as they assembled. "We had taken the first step," he notes, "it wasn't so bad, and we were still alive."[16]

Despite the fact that military reports showed no alerts had been issued to Soviet forces anywhere in the world, the president felt it necessary to proceed with preparations for a possible blockade of Berlin. American U-2 planes were now routinely flying over Cuba to take photographs of the missile sites, flying lower to the ground (barely above the tops of the trees) in order to produce sharper images. ExComm began to discuss what would happen if one of these U-2s were shot down. Military leaders argued forcefully that American troops must be defended in the event of an attack. Finally, the group agreed that if a U-2 were shot down, American bombers and fighters would destroy a missile site, but only upon the direct order of the president. "By this time, the relaxed, lighter mood had completely disappeared," Robert Kennedy noted. "It had taken only a few minutes."[17] The president was deeply concerned that a mistake would be made in that tense atmosphere.

In those days before satellite imagery, the pilots flew in pairs over the missile sites. Their planes were equipped with six cameras underneath the plane: one large camera beneath the cockpit, four smaller cameras mounted at different angles further back, and then a tail camera. Because film was limited, the pilots waited until the last minute to switch on the cameras.

MISSILE ERECTOR

CABLE

MISSILE SHELTER TENT

TRACKED PRIME MOVERS

OXIDIZER TANK TRAILERS

FUEL TANK TRAILERS

As Kennedy waited for the Soviets to respond to his demands, U.S. airplanes equipped with cameras flew over Cuba to gather more information. These reconnaissance missions produced photographs that were clearer and more detailed than earlier images, and confirmed the presence of Soviet missiles and erector sites.

Zooming over the missile site, the pilots had approximately 10 seconds to take the critical photographs.

What they discovered was that the missile erectors—which had been recorded in those first alarming images—had now been covered in canvas and were connected by cables to a command post hidden in the trees. Long tents, several hundred yards from the erectors, contained the actual missiles. A large, hangar-like building was being built out of white slabs; photo interpreters identified these structures as bunkers for the nuclear warheads.

Later that evening, the president signed a two-page proclamation formally instituting the quarantine. The quarantine force would consist of 16 destroyers, 3 cruisers, an antisubmarine aircraft carrier, and 6 other ships, with more than 100 additional ships in reserve. Ships carrying food and oil would be allowed through; any suspected of transporting offensive weapons would be stopped and searched. The president and his advisers had debated what steps should be taken if a Soviet ship failed to stop when ordered. If a ship refused to stop, the navy was to try to avoid sinking the ship and killing Soviet troops if at all possible. Instead, the president ordered that the navy should first fire at the ship's rudder or propeller.

Secretary of Defense Robert McNamara was dispatched to the section of the Pentagon where the navy was overseeing the enforcement of the blockade. McNamara was mindful of the president's concern that a small incident or misunderstanding, perhaps between an American and Russian sailor, could quickly lead to nuclear war in this tense atmosphere. McNamara wanted to ensure that he—and the president—were receiving minute-by-minute information as the quarantine got under way. He asked numerous detailed questions about how the navy would stop the first Soviet ship to attempt to cross the quarantine line, repeatedly stressing that no shots were to be fired without his express permission and thoroughly angering the chief of naval operations.

Late that evening, Robert Kennedy drove to the Soviet Embassy to meet with Ambassador Anatoly Dobrynin. He informed him of the president's deep anger over the misinformation he had been given, at the repeated false assurances he had been given that the Soviets would not place offensive missiles in Cuba. Dobrynin could only repeat that, as far as he knew, there were no missiles in Cuba; perhaps the American information was wrong.

As he was leaving, Robert Kennedy asked what instructions had been given to the captains of Soviet ships headed for Cuba.

The ambassador replied that, as far as he knew, the Soviet captains would ignore "unlawful demands to stop or be searched on the open sea."

"I don't know how this will end," Robert Kennedy replied, "but we intend to stop your ships."[18]

Yes or No

On Wednesday, October 24, the members of ExComm gathered at the White House to review intelligence connected to the quarantine. These reports showed that some 22 Soviet ships were currently headed for Cuba, including several that were thought to be carrying missiles.

The quarantine barrier stretched along a 500-mile (805-km) radius from the eastern tip of Cuba. Two of the Soviet ships, the *Yuri Gagarin* and the *Kimovsk*, were nearing the barrier. In between them was a Soviet submarine. The *Kimovsk* had exceptionally long cargo hatches—hatches that were long enough to contain missiles. According to the rules of engagement, the Soviet ships would be destroyed if they failed to comply with U.S. Navy instructions. In less than an hour, the two ships—and their submarine escort—would reach the barrier, and the navy would then need to respond.

After Kennedy ordered the naval quarantine, ExComm received intelligence informing them of 22 Soviet naval vessels headed toward Cuba. Some of these ships were thought to be carrying additional Soviet missiles to the Caribbean island.

"I think these few minutes were the time of gravest concern for the President," Robert Kennedy later wrote. "Was the world on the brink of a holocaust? Was it our error? A mistake? Was there something further that should have been done? Or not done? . . . One thousand miles away in the vast expanse of the Atlantic Ocean the final decisions were going to be made in the next few minutes. President Kennedy had initiated the course of events, but he no longer had control over them. He would have to wait—we would have to wait."[1]

Suddenly, the CIA director was handed a message, which he quickly shared with those gathered. The Soviet ships had all stopped or reversed course.

"We're eyeball to eyeball, and the other fellow just blinked,"[2] Secretary of State Dean Rusk said to the relieved men in the room.

Later reports showed that the ships had changed course several hours earlier, but the intelligence had failed to be properly conveyed up the chain of command. Khrushchev may have blinked, but it took nearly 30 hours for the "blink" to become apparent to the decision makers in Washington.[3]

The apparent victory was short-lived. Late that night, the president received a grim letter from Chairman Khrushchev. "In presenting us with these conditions," Khrushchev wrote, "you have flung a challenge at us. Who asked you to do this? By what right did you do this?" Khrushchev accused Kennedy of taking action based on "hatred for the Cuban people and its government" and also out of consideration for the midterm elections scheduled for November. The letter also accused the United States of "outright banditry" and "the folly of degenerate imperialism." The letter concluded by stating that the captains of Soviet ships would not be instructed to observe the blockade. "We will not simply be bystanders with regard to piratical acts by American ships on the high seas," it said. "We will then be forced on our part to take the measures we consider necessary and adequate in order to protect our rights. We have everything necessary to do so."[4]

CONFRONTATION AT THE UNITED NATIONS

The world now knew that the United States and the Soviet Union were engaged in a confrontation, but there were no 24-hour news channels broadcasting continuous footage from the quarantine line or the missile sites in Cuba. Instead, the first opportunity for a television broadcast of the confrontation between the two nations came during a meeting of the United Nations Security Council on Thursday, October 25.

The U.S. ambassador to the United Nations was Adlai Stevenson. Stevenson and the president had a prickly relationship. Stevenson had not selected John Kennedy as his vice presidential nominee during his own unsuccessful presidential campaign in 1956, and he had assisted Lyndon Johnson against Kennedy in the 1960 campaign to become the Democratic candidate for president. At the time, Stevenson had been one of the most popular Democrats in the country, and his support was considered important. Kennedy had appointed him as UN ambassador as a way to appease his supporters but also to place him in what was viewed as a less prominent post than other cabinet positions.

Stevenson had been present at one of the earlier discussions focusing on an appropriate response to the missiles and had angered many in the room when he proposed that the missiles in Turkey and Italy be used as a negotiating tool—that the president extend an offer to withdraw the NATO missiles in Turkey and Italy in exchange for Soviet withdrawal of the missiles in Cuba. The president and his brother, Robert, both worried that Stevenson was not tough enough to stand up to the Soviets in a confrontation at the UN.

Early that morning, the president had sent to Stevenson a copy of the latest, threatening letter from Khrushchev that he had received the day before, undoubtedly to give him a picture of the current status of efforts to negotiate with the Soviets. Late that afternoon, the UN ambassador entered the Security Council.

The Security Council chamber was a smaller meeting place than the larger General Assembly. The round table featured space for only 20 chairs. That day, anticipating a possible confrontation, UN staff and diplomats had crowded into the room, standing near the doors, to witness the discussion.

That afternoon, the meeting was being chaired by Valerian Zorin, the Soviet ambassador to the UN. Lacking clear instructions from Khrushchev, Zorin's strategy was simply to deny

During a televised meeting of the United Nations Security Council, U.S. ambassador Adlai Stevenson *(second from right)* confronted the Soviet delegate, Valerian Zorin *(first on left)*, about the Soviet missiles in Cuba. When Zorin refused to answer, Stevenson presented photographic proof of the Soviet missile sites in Cuba.

the existence of the missiles in Cuba. The continued denials angered Stevenson, who was seated four chairs away from the Soviet ambassador.

Finally, Stevenson asked for the floor to pose one question: "Do you, Ambassador Zorin, deny that the U.S.S.R. has placed, and is placing, medium and intermediate range missiles and sites in Cuba? Yes or no—don't wait for the translation—yes or no."

When Zorin testily replied that he was not in a courtroom and did not wish to be addressed in that manner, Stevenson swiftly answered, "You are in the courtroom of world opinion right now, and you can answer yes or no. You have denied that they exist, and I want to know if I have understood you correctly."

"You will receive your answer in due course," Zorin replied through the translator. "Do not worry."

"I am prepared to wait for my answer until hell freezes over, if that is your decision,"[5] Stevenson firmly replied.

Stevenson then called for a pair of wooden easels to be set up at the back of the room. On them was placed the photographic evidence, demonstrating to those in the Security Council chamber and the television audience that the missiles were indeed in position in Cuba. As those in the room craned their necks to see the images, Zorin ignored the easels and instead busied himself writing notes on a pad in front of him.

THE FIRST SHIP

By Friday, October 26, the president determined that another demonstration of U.S. will was needed. He had announced the naval blockade four days earlier, and no ships had been boarded. One Soviet oil tanker, the *Bucharest*, had crossed the blockade line after assuring naval officers that it had no offensive weapons on board.

The president decided that the quarantine now needed to be actively enforced. The ship selected was the freighter *Marucla*, which was sailing to Cuba with a declared cargo of spare truck parts, paper, and sulfur. The ship, although chartered by the Soviet Union, had a largely Greek crew. It was highly unlikely that the ship would be carrying Soviet missiles, but still it was determined that the ship should be boarded and searched to demonstrate U.S. resolve.

The *Marucla* was signaled to stop and prepare for a search. The ship selected to enforce the quarantine was the American destroyer *Joseph P. Kennedy, Jr.*, named for the president's late brother and a ship on which his brother Robert had served in 1946. The instructions were clear—there should be no firing across the bow, nor any threatening actions. Instead, the *Marucla* was signaled by flag and flashing light to prepare for an inspection. The Greek crew hospitably offered American searchers coffee as they began the search. No missiles were found, and the *Marucla* was allowed to continue to Cuba.

NIKITA KHRUSHCHEV

Nikita Khrushchev was born in a Ukrainian province in April 1894 to a family of peasants. Unlike many of the Soviet leaders who preceded him, he was forced to work his way up from very humble beginnings, working first as a pipe fitter before joining the Russian Communist Party the year after a revolution had overthrown the Russian royal family.

Khrushchev served in the Red Army through Russia's civil war and then in struggles with Polish troops. He then attended several of the new Soviet schools before joining the Communist Party as a full-time employee in 1925, specializing in advising on the conditions in mines and factories. He gained a reputation as an effective party organizer and rose quickly within the Communist headquarters, becoming first secretary of Moscow in 1935 and a member of the Politburo (the principal policy making organization in the Soviet Union) in 1939.

Khrushchev proved especially skilled at maintaining a good relationship with the then Soviet leader, Joseph Stalin. When Stalin's health began to fail, Khrushchev quickly moved to consolidate his own power base by establishing close ties with local Communist Party leaders. He successfully challenged Stalin's hand-picked successor, Georgy Malenkov, to become leader of the Soviet Union in 1955, after Stalin's death.

In 1956, Khrushchev stunned many in his party by publicly criticizing his predecessor, Stalin, in a speech that lasted six hours. Up

As this first enforcement of the blockade passed relatively uneventfully, the president was receiving an intelligence briefing that signaled that the Cuban Missile Crisis was entering a new phase. The director of the National Photographic Interpretation Center had brought for the president's review

until then, it had been forbidden to say anything negative about Stalin (who had ruled the country for 25 years).

Khrushchev set ambitious goals for his country, particularly in agricultural production. He gained a reputation as a brash and often unpredictable leader on the world stage. He honestly believed that Communism was a superior political system that would ultimately win out over democracy, and he used dramatic events to demonstrate that belief. Under Khrushchev, the Soviet Union launched the first satellite, *Sputnik*, soon followed by the first dog, first man, and first woman in space. Khrushchev flew to a summit in London in a half-completed prototype of a passenger jet, demonstrating the advanced state of Soviet aviation (at a time before England had a passenger jet of its own).

In an effort to ensure the spread of Communism, Khrushchev encouraged the increase of Soviet aid to countries in Africa, Asia, and Latin America. He famously banged one of his shoes on the podium during a speech to the UN General Assembly.

His actions during the Cuban Missile Crisis would ultimately lead to his ousting in 1964. The cause was in large part the embarrassment brought about by the forced withdrawal of Soviet missiles from Cuba. He died of a heart attack in 1971 and was the only Soviet leader not to be buried in the Kremlin.

the latest photos taken by U.S. Navy Crusader jets flying low over western and central Cuba. These low-level images provided far greater detail, showing the unmistakable signs of missile shelter tents, concrete launch stands, fuel trucks, and bunkers for nuclear warheads. The images also contained alarming news. In one section of central Cuba, there was a camp with numerous tanks, electronics vans, armored personnel carriers, and more than 100 tents. Analysis of the photos had revealed that this was a Soviet, not Cuban, military camp. The photos also showed a 35-foot-long (10.7-m) object next to a radar truck—a Free Rocket Over Ground, or FROG. This type of missile could be used against invading troops and could be either conventional or nuclear. The photos suggested that, in addition to the nuclear missiles targeting the United States from Cuba, the Soviet Union now had large numbers of combat troops stationed in Cuba, and they were equipped with short-range missiles (possibly nuclear tipped) that could be used to destroy an American invading force.[6]

The president was increasingly convinced that a diplomatic solution to the crisis might not be possible. The photos suggested that the Soviets were preparing for war in Cuba. Robert Kennedy noted in his memoirs, "Each hour the situation grew steadily more serious. The feeling grew that this cup was not going to pass and that a direct military confrontation between the two great nuclear powers was inevitable. . . . If the Russians continued to build up their missile strength, military force would be the only alternative."[7]

President Kennedy ordered the State Department to begin to make plans for a type of civil government that could be established in Cuba should the United States need to invade and occupy the island. Secretary of Defense McNamara reminded the president that, particularly after the photo intelligence provided by the U.S. Navy photos, an invasion would result in very heavy casualties.

"We are going to have to face the fact," the president replied, "that if we do invade, by the time we get to these [missile] sites, after a very bloody fight, they will be pointed at us. And we must further accept the possibility that when military hostilities first begin, those missiles will be fired."[8]

Conflicting
Letters

Late on that Friday afternoon, a messenger arrived at the
U.S. Embassy in Moscow, carrying a long letter for President Kennedy that was signed "N. Khrushchev" in purple
ink. Normally, such correspondence would have come from
the Soviet Foreign Ministry; the courier explained that he
was told to bring the letter directly to the embassy. The letter
seemed to have been written in haste; corrections were made
in purple ink, with words crossed out and replaced. Embassy
experts were quickly ordered to translate the letter from Russian into English. Some 12 hours later, it was transmitted by
teletype to Washington.

With so much at stake, the delays in communication were
particularly dangerous. Phone communication was not yet fully
global, and connections were of high quality in certain parts of
the world but severely lacking in others. There were no faxes or

When Fidel Castro (*left*) and his forces established a Communist government in Cuba, they quickly gained an ally in the Soviet Union. The two countries became trading partners, and Khrushchev (*right*) believed building a military base on the island would provide protection to both countries against U.S. aggression.

e-mail. President Kennedy could phone the British prime minister but not the leader of the Soviet Union. Communications between the Pentagon and the warships enforcing the blockade could be delayed by six to eight hours. If the Soviet ambassador in Washington wanted to communicate with Moscow, the message had to be encoded. Next, the Soviet Embassy contacted the

(*continues on page 64*)

THE FIRST LETTER

On the evening of October 26, 1962, a letter from Chairman Khrushchev to President Kennedy arrived at the State Department. The letter lacked the normal diplomatic polish and neatness, and it had been signed in purple ink. In addition to suggesting a way out of the crisis, the letter revealed a Soviet leader struggling with the stress of the situation, as this excerpt reveals:

> I see, Mr. President, that you too are not devoid of a sense of anxiety for the fate of the world understanding, and of what war entails. What would a war give you? You are threatening us with war. But you well know that the very least which you would receive in reply would be that you would experience the same consequences as those which you sent us. And that must be clear to us, people invested with authority, trust, and responsibility. We must not succumb to intoxication and petty passions, regardless of whether elections are impending in this or that country, or not impending. These are all transient things, but if indeed war should break out, then it would not be in our power to stop it, for such is the logic of war. I have participated in two wars and know that war ends when it has rolled through cities and villages, everywhere sowing death and destruction. . . .
>
> In the name of the Soviet Government and the Soviet people, I assure you that your conclusions regarding offensive weapons on Cuba are groundless. It is apparent from what you have written me that our conceptions are different on this score, or rather, we have different estimates of these or those military means. Indeed, in reality, the same forms of weapons can have different interpretations.
>
> You are a military man and, I hope, will understand me. Let us take for example a simple cannon. What sort of means is this:

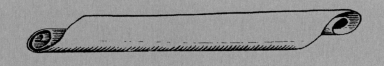

offensive or defensive? A cannon is a defensive means if it is set up to defend boundaries or a fortified area. But if one concentrates artillery, and adds to it the necessary number of troops, then the same cannons do become an offensive means, because they prepare and clear the way for infantry to attack. The same happens with missile-nuclear weapons as well, with any type of this weapon. . . .

Consequently, Mr. President, let us show good sense. I assure you that on those ships, which are bound for Cuba, there are no weapons at all. The weapons which were necessary for the defense of Cuba are already there. I do not want to say that there were not any shipments of weapons at all. No, there were such shipments. But now Cuba has already received the necessary means of defense.

I don't know whether you can understand me and believe me. But I should like to have you believe in yourself and to agree that one cannot give way to passions; it is necessary to control them. And in what direction are events now developing? If you stop the vessels, then, as you yourself know, that would be piracy. If we started to do that with regard to your ships, then you would also be as indignant as we and the whole world now are. One cannot give another interpretation to such actions, because one cannot legalize lawlessness. If this were permitted, then there would be no peace, there would also be no peaceful coexistence. We should then be forced to put into effect the necessary measures of a defensive character to protect our interests in accordance with international law. Why should this be done? To what would all this lead? . . .

(continues)

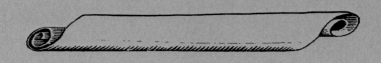

(continued)

If assurances were given by the President and the Government of the United States that the USA itself would not participate in an attack on Cuba and would restrain others from actions of this sort, if you would recall your fleet, this would immediately change everything. . . . Then, too, the question of armaments would disappear, since, if there is no threat, then armaments are a burden for every people. Then too, the question of the destruction, not only of the armaments which you call offensive, but of all other armaments as well, would look different. . . .

Let us therefore show statesmanlike wisdom. I propose: We, for our part, will declare that our ships, bound for Cuba, will not carry any kind of armaments. You would declare that the United States will not invade Cuba with its forces and will not support any sort of forces which might intend to carry out an invasion of Cuba. Then the necessity for the presence of our military specialists in Cuba would disappear.

"Telegram from the Embassy in the Soviet Union to the Department of State, October 26, 1962, 7 P.M." Kennedy-Khrushchev Exchanges, U.S. Department of State. http://www.state.gov/www/about_state/history/volume_vi/exchanges.html.

(continued from page 61)
local office of Western Union (the company that handled sending telegrams long distances). Western Union sent a young man on a bicycle to collect the telegram who would then pedal back to the Western Union office, where the coded message would be sent to the Kremlin by telegraph.

This latest letter from Khrushchev finally came over the State Department wires on Friday night. Analysts studied it, believing that it had been written by the Soviet leader himself. Secretary of State Dean Rusk thought the letter revealed that Khrushchev was "disturbed" and "trying to find a way to get out"[1] of the crisis.

In the letter, Khrushchev continued to insist that the missiles were only to defend Cuba. Late in the letter, however, Khrushchev suggested that there was a solution to the crisis. If the United States withdrew its ships and promised not to attack Cuba, there would no longer be a need for Soviet "military specialists" on the island. Comparing the crisis to a knot tied in a rope that was tightening the harder the rope was pulled, he said, "A moment may come when that knot will be tied so tight that even he who tied it will not have the strength to untie it, and then it will be necessary to cut that knot, and what that would mean is not for me to explain to you, because you yourself understand perfectly of what terrible forces our countries dispose. Consequently, if there is no intention to tighten that knot and thereby to doom the world to the catastrophe of thermonuclear war, then let us not only relax the forces pulling on the ends of the rope, let us take measures to untie that knot. We are ready for this."[2]

ExComm members read and reread the letter. Finally, they decided that the State Department would analyze it further and then offer a proposal on how best to respond. A meeting was scheduled for the next morning.

A SECOND LETTER

On Saturday morning, October 27, as he was preparing to leave for the ExComm meeting, Robert Kennedy received a disturbing letter from the director of the Federal Bureau of Investigation, J. Edgar Hoover. Hoover reported that he had been given information that certain Soviet personnel in New York were

(continues on page 68)

THE SECOND LETTER

On October 27, 1962, President Kennedy received a second letter from Chairman Khrushchev. This letter was more polished and formal than the letter sent by Khrushchev the day before, and it included demands for the removal of U.S. missiles in Turkey, as this excerpt reveals:

> You wish to ensure the security of your country, and this is understandable. But Cuba, too, wants the same thing; all countries want to maintain their security. But how are we, the Soviet Union, our Government, to assess your actions which are expressed in the fact that you have surrounded the Soviet Union with military bases; surrounded our allies with military bases; placed military bases literally around our country; and stationed your missile armaments there? This is no secret. Responsible American personages openly declare that it is so. Your missiles are located in Britain, are located in Italy, and are aimed against us. Your missiles are located in Turkey.
>
> You are disturbed over Cuba. You say that this disturbs you because it is 90 miles by sea from the coast of the United States of America. But Turkey adjoins us; our sentries patrol back and forth and see each other. Do you consider, then, that you have the right to demand security for your own country and the removal of the weapons you call offensive, but do not accord the same right to us? You have placed destructive missile weapons, which you call offensive, in Turkey, literally next to us. How then can recognition of our equal military capacities be reconciled with such unequal relations between our great states? This is irreconcilable. . . .
>
> I think it would be possible to end the controversy quickly and normalize the situation, and then the people could breathe more easily, considering that statesmen charged with responsibility are

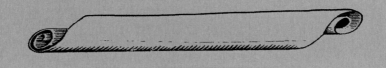

of sober mind and have an awareness of their responsibility com-
bined with the ability to solve complex questions and not bring
things to a military catastrophe.

I therefore make this proposal: We are willing to remove from
Cuba the means which you regard as offensive. We are willing
to carry this out and to make this pledge in the United Nations.
Your representatives will make a declaration to the effect that the
United States, for its part, considering the uneasiness and anxiety
of the Soviet State, will remove its analogous means from Turkey.
Let us reach agreement as to the period of time needed by you
and by us to bring this about. And, after that, persons entrusted
by the United Nations Security Council could inspect on the spot
the fulfillment of the pledges made. Of course, the permission of
the Governments of Cuba and of Turkey is necessary for the entry
into those countries of these representatives and for the inspection of the fulfillment of the pledge made by each side. Of course
it would be best if these representatives enjoyed the confidence
of the Security Council, as well as yours and mine—both the
United States and the Soviet Union—and also that of Turkey and
Cuba. I do not think it would be difficult to select people who
would enjoy the trust and respect of all parties concerned.

We, in making this pledge, in order to give satisfaction and
hope of the peoples of Cuba and Turkey and to strengthen their
confidence in their security, will make a statement within the
framework of the Security Council to the effect that the Soviet
Government gives a solemn promise to respect the inviolability of
the borders and sovereignty of Turkey, not to interfere in its internal affairs, not to invade Turkey, not to make available our

(continues)

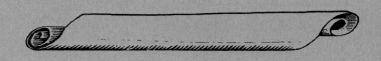

(continued)

territory as a bridgehead for such an invasion, and that it would also restrain those who contemplate committing aggression against Turkey, either from the territory of the Soviet Union or from the territory of Turkey's other neighboring states.

The United States Government will make a similar statement within the framework of the Security Council regarding Cuba. It will declare that the United States will respect the inviolability of Cuba's borders and its sovereignty, will pledge not to interfere in its internal affairs, not to invade Cuba itself or make its territory available as a bridgehead for such an invasion, and will also restrain those who might contemplate committing aggression against Cuba, either from the territory of the United States or from the territory of Cuba's other neighboring states.

Of course, for this we would have to come to an agreement with you and specify a certain time limit. Let us agree to some period of time, but without unnecessary delay—say within two or three weeks, not longer than a month.

"Message from Chairman Khrushchev to President Kennedy (the Second Letter), October 27, 1962." Mount Holyoke College. http://www.mtholyoke.edu/acad/intrel/nikita3.htm.

(continued from page 65)

preparing to destroy all sensitive documents on the basis that the United States would soon be taking military action against Cuba or Soviet ships. This would mean war. Robert Kennedy reflected on the contradiction as he drove to the White

House—why were the Soviets preparing for war if they were anxious to find a solution to the crisis? How did this behavior fit with the letter from Khrushchev the day before?[3]

His concern proved justified at the ExComm meeting when President Kennedy was handed a new letter from Chairman Khrushchev, which had apparently been broadcast a short time ago on Radio Moscow. The letter was quite different from the one that had been received the night before. More formal in tone, the letter mentioned the NATO missiles stationed in Britain, Italy, and Turkey that targeted the Soviet Union.

"You are disturbed over Cuba," the letter read. "You say that this disturbs you because it is 90 miles by sea from the coast of the United States of America. But Turkey adjoins us; our sentries patrol back and forth and see each other. Do you consider, then, that you have the right to demand security for your own country and the removal of the weapons you call offensive, but do not accord the same right to us?"[4]

Robert Kennedy described this as the most difficult 24 hours of the missile crisis.[5] Adding to the tension, Secretary of Defense McNamara had received reports that the Soviets were working throughout the day and night to complete work on the missile sites.

President Kennedy quickly understood the difficult situation into which he had been placed with this new letter. The previous year, he had suggested removing the Turkish missiles because they were outdated and no longer militarily useful. Most people would view the Soviet demand for the removal of missiles in Turkey in exchange for the removal of the Cuban missiles as a reasonable demand. If the United States refused, the president said, "I think you're going to find it very difficult to explain why we are going to take hostile military action in Cuba. . . . I think we've got a very tough one here."[6]

The members of ExComm debated. Had both letters come from Khrushchev? If so, why had he changed his mind and issued more demands in the second letter?

A Soviet air missile shot down an American U-2 airplane and killed its pilot, Major Rudolf Anderson Jr., during the crisis. Anderson's death put additional pressure on Kennedy and ExComm to resolve tensions before they escalated into full-out war.

"The change in the language and tenor of the letters from Khrushchev indicated confusion within the Soviet Union," Attorney General Robert Kennedy wrote. "But there was confusion among us as well. At that moment, not knowing exactly what to suggest, some recommended writing to Khrushchev and asking him to clarify his two letters. There was no clear course of action. Yet we realized that, as we sat there, the work was proceeding on the missile sites in Cuba, and we now had the additional consideration that if we destroyed these sites and began an invasion, the door was clearly open for the Soviet Union to take reciprocal action against Turkey."[7]

The Joint Chiefs of Staff joined the ExComm meeting in the afternoon. They felt that the letters were proof of what they had suspected all along—the naval blockade was too weak a response and would prove ineffective. They argued for a massive air strike and invasion of Cuba, beginning in two days, on Monday, October 29.

As this approach was being debated, the meeting was interrupted with sad news: A U-2 plane on a photo-reconnaissance mission over Cuba had been shot down by a Soviet surface-to-air missile. Its pilot, Major Rudolf Anderson Jr., had been killed. The already tense climate increased dramatically. "There was sympathy for Major Anderson and his family," Robert Kennedy recalled. "There was the knowledge that we had to take military action to protect our pilots. There was the realization that the Soviet Union and Cuba apparently were preparing to do battle. And there was the feeling that the noose was tightening on all of us, on Americans, on mankind, and that the bridges to escape were crumbling."[8]

Final Attempt

President Kennedy was increasingly aware that a slight miscalculation, a small mistake, could result in events quickly moving beyond his control. A second American U-2 pilot on a routine mission had that very day strayed into Soviet airspace and been briefly pursued by Soviet fighters before safely returning to Alaska. The president had ordered those flying missions canceled, in an effort to avoid a tense confrontation, but clearly the message had not been transmitted to all pilots. That pilot could easily have been shot down; Major Anderson, flying over Cuba, had been shot down.

He decided to make one last effort at negotiation. Robert Kennedy and Ted Sorensen, among others, had suggested that the president simply ignore the second letter from Chairman Khrushchev and instead reply to the first letter, the letter that was received on Friday night. He decided to make his response public, in part for reasons of speed and also to help influence world opinion—to make it clear that the United States was pursuing all diplomatic channels first.

Those working on the appropriate response did not realize that, at the same time, Cuba's leader, Fidel Castro, was sending his own message to Khrushchev through the Soviet ambassador in Cuba. In that letter, predicting that the United States would invade Cuba within the next 72 hours, Castro urged the Soviet leader to fire its missiles should the United States begin an air attack and invasion.

"The Soviet Union must never allow the circumstances in which the imperialists could launch the first nuclear strike against it," Castro wrote. "I tell you this because I believe the imperialists' aggressiveness is extremely dangerous and if they actually carry out the brutal act of invading Cuba in violation of international law and morality, that would be the moment to eliminate such danger forever through an act of clear legitimate defense, however harsh and terrible the solution would be, for there is no other."[1]

KENNEDY RESPONDS

The final draft of the official U.S. response, the result of work by Attorney General Robert Kennedy and speechwriter Ted Sorensen, was approved by the president later that day. The letter noted that the president had authorized his representatives to work with the UN and the Soviets to ensure "a permanent solution to the Cuban problem along the lines suggested in your letter of October 26th."[2] If Khrushchev would dismantle and remove all offensive weapons in Cuba, the United States would halt the quarantine and agree not to invade Cuba.

The only reference to Khrushchev's second letter came in a simple, vague phrase: "The effect of such a settlement on easing world tensions would enable us to work toward a more general arrangement regarding 'other armaments,' as proposed in your second letter which you made public."[3]

With the help of his speechwriter, Ted Sorenson (*right*), President Kennedy (*left*) replied to Khrushchev's letter with his own demands and concessions. Robert Kennedy personally delivered the president's response to the Soviet ambassador.

The president decided that the message would be delivered personally by his brother, the attorney general, to the Soviet ambassador, Anatoly Dobrynin. He wanted his brother to specifically convey his great concern over the worsening crisis and also to give Dobrynin a verbal warning: If there was no reply to this message by Monday, two days from then, the United States would begin a military action against Cuba. He also wanted to make sure that the missiles in Turkey were not an obstacle to agreement but also not an excuse for additional bargaining.

Robert Kennedy was to convey to the Soviet ambassador the information that the missiles in Turkey were soon scheduled for withdrawal, but this information must remain confidential. If the Soviet Union publicized this fact, the offer for a peaceful resolution to the crisis would be withdrawn.

Robert Kennedy phoned Dobrynin and arranged for a meeting at his office at the Department of Justice at 7:45 that night. In his large, dimly lit office, lined with artwork by his children, Robert Kennedy grimly told the Soviet ambassador that the president did not want a military conflict, but the shooting down of the American U-2 plane represented a serious event. Certain decisions were going to be made within the next 12 to 24 hours, he explained. If the Cubans shot at any additional planes, the Americans would return fire.

Part of the attorney general's aim was to ensure that the ambassador understood specifically what was happening at the White House. The military was demanding that the president "respond to fire with fire," Kennedy explained. If the Soviet bases in Cuba were not removed, the United States would bomb them—resulting in the loss of many lives, including Soviet citizens—in which case the Soviet Union would inevitably respond. "A real war will begin," Kennedy warned, "in which millions of Americans and Russians will die. We want to avoid that any way we can."[4]

He then explained the contents of the letter the president had prepared for Chairman Khrushchev: The quarantine would be ended and the United States would agree not to invade Cuba if the Soviet Union dismantled its missile bases there. The ambassador asked about Turkey—a reference to Khrushchev's demand in his second letter, the one that the president had decided to ignore. Robert Kennedy outlined the plan that his brother and the other members of ExComm had finally accepted: The missiles in Turkey would be withdrawn within four to five months, but this plan was not to be made public. The missiles had been placed there as part of a NATO agreement; the United States could not appear to be acting without first consulting its NATO allies. The Soviet Union must respond to this final plan by the next day. "There's very little time left,"[5] Robert Kennedy warned. The meeting lasted 15 minutes.

The Soviet ambassador quickly sent a coded message back to Moscow, outlining the discussion. At the end, perhaps to emphasize the seriousness of the discussion, he added his personal observation: "I should say that during our meeting R. Kennedy was very upset; in any case, I've never seen him like this before. . . . He didn't even try to get into fights on various subjects, as he usually does, and only persistently returned to one topic: time is of the essence and we shouldn't miss the chance."[6]

PLANNING FOR THE WORST

Robert Kennedy immediately returned to the White House to brief his brother on the meeting. It was late Saturday evening. There was still great uncertainty about how the Soviet Union would respond to this latest message. At least one member of ExComm had suggested that, now that Khrushchev had been given warning that an air strike was imminent without an agreement that the missiles would be removed, he might choose to strike first.

The White House was considered a primary target for Soviet missiles. Key White House staff members had been given specific instructions about what they were to do in the event of an attack. Special pink identification cards were issued to the president's closest advisers; they would be evacuated with the president by helicopter to an underground bunker in West Virginia if an attack was thought to be imminent. The helicopter crew had been issued protective gear and rescue equipment, should they need to retrieve the president after a nuclear attack. To ensure the survival of the U.S. government in the event of nuclear war, the plan included the evacuation of cabinet secretaries, Supreme Court justices, and other senior federal

In the event of a Soviet nuclear attack, plans were implemented to protect White House staff members and the president. Equipment was prepared and personnel were trained to transport the president to a secret bunker in West Virginia (*above*).

officials. The underground facilities included an emergency broadcasting network, a hospital, an emergency power plant, decontamination chambers, and even a presidential suite. Congress had its own underground bunker, located beneath the Greenbrier Hotel, a luxury resort in West Virginia. Plans had even been drawn up to rescue certain important documents and treasures, such as the Declaration of Independence.[7]

In a final meeting of ExComm at nine o'clock that Saturday evening, the president approved a plan to call up 24 air reserve squadrons. If American planes were attacked on Sunday and there was not a positive response from Khrushchev that day, the United States would bomb the missile sites in Cuba. The president would review the air strike plans Sunday morning. The meeting included a discussion of what form of government could be set up in Cuba in the event of an invasion and how the United States would respond to what was viewed as an almost inevitable Soviet action in Europe should the president order the air strike. The meeting finally ended near midnight, and the president sent his advisers home to spend that night with their families.

The Crisis Ends

At 9:00 A.M. on Sunday, October 28, 1962, the White House learned that Radio Moscow was broadcasting a message. Chairman Khrushchev was about to make an important statement.

Some members of ExComm heard the news and feared that the message would be Khrushchev's rejection of the latest offer. In that case, an air strike would be ordered.

As the message began, it was quickly translated and transmitted to National Security Adviser McGeorge Bundy, the man who had first alerted the president to the crisis. Breakfasting at the White House, he reviewed the hastily scrawled phrases from the translation and then rushed to inform the president.

(continues on page 82)

"WE ARE PREPARED TO REACH AGREEMENT"

On October 28, 1962, Radio Moscow broadcast the text of a message from Chairman Khrushchev to President Kennedy, a message that signaled that, after 13 days, the Cuban Missile Crisis was at an end. This excerpt is taken from the English translation of that message:

Dear Mr. President:

I have received your message of October 27. I express my satisfaction and thank you for the sense of proportion you have displayed and for realization of the responsibility which now devolves on you for the preservation of the peace of the world.

I regard with great understanding your concern and the concern of the United States people in connection with the fact that the weapons you describe as offensive are formidable weapons indeed. Both you and we understand what kind of weapons these are.

In order to eliminate as rapidly as possible the conflict which endangers the cause of peace, to give an assurance to all people who crave peace, and to reassure the American people, who, I am certain, also want peace, as do the people of the Soviet Union, the Soviet Government, in addition to earlier instructions on the discontinuation of further work on weapons construction sites, has given a new order to dismantle the arms which you described as offensive, and to crate and return them to the Soviet Union. . . .

I regard with respect and trust the statement you made in your message of October 27, 1962, that there would be no attack, no invasion of Cuba, and not only on the part of the United States, but also on the part of other nations of the Western Hemisphere, as you said in your same message. Then the motives which induced us to render assistance of such a kind to Cuba disappear.

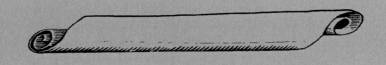

It is for this reason that we instructed our officers—these means as I had already informed you earlier are in the hands of the Soviet officers—to take appropriate measures to discontinue construction of the aforementioned facilities, to dismantle them, and to return them to the Soviet Union. As I had informed you in the letter of October 27, we are prepared to reach agreement to enable United Nations Representatives to verify the dismantling of these means.

Thus in view of the assurance you have given and our instructions on dismantling, there is every condition for eliminating the present conflict.

I note with satisfaction that you have responded to the desire I expressed with regard to elimination of the aforementioned dangerous situation, as well as with regard to providing conditions for a more thoughtful appraisal of the internal situation, fraught as it is with great dangers in our age of thermonuclear weapons, rocketry, spaceships, global rockets, and other deadly weapons. All people are interested in insuring peace.

Therefore, vested with trust and great responsibility, we must not allow the situation to become aggravated and must stamp out the centers where a dangerous situation fraught with grave consequences to the cause of peace has arisen. If we, together with you, and with the assistance of other people of good will, succeed in eliminating this tense atmosphere, we should also make certain that no other dangerous conflicts which could lead to a world nuclear catastrophe would arise.

"Letter from Chairman Khrushchev to President Kennedy, October 28, 1962." John F. Kennedy Presidential Library and Museum. http://www .jfklibrary.org/cmc.

(continued from page 79)

"In order to eliminate as rapidly as possible the conflict which endangers the cause of peace, to give an assurance to all people who crave peace, and to reassure the American people, who, I am certain, also want peace, as do the people of the Soviet Union, the Soviet Government, in addition to earlier instructions on the discontinuation of further work on weapons construction sites, has given a new order to dismantle the arms which you described as offensive, and to crate and return them to the Soviet Union,"[1] Khrushchev's message stated.

The announcement sparked joyous relief in the members of ExComm. Bundy noted, "It was a very beautiful morning, and it had suddenly become many times more beautiful. . . . We all felt that the world had changed for the better."[2]

Bundy gave the full text of the message to President Kennedy, who was preparing to leave for Mass. "I feel like a new man," the president replied in relief. "Thank God it's all over."[3] He announced that an ExComm meeting would be held at 11:30, explaining that he and his wife were now going to church, and he advised everyone else to do the same.[4]

Later that morning, Robert Kennedy received a message from the Soviet ambassador, requesting a meeting. Ambassador Dobrynin confirmed what the radio message had stated—Khrushchev had agreed to dismantle and withdraw the missiles. He added that Khrushchev "wanted to send his best wishes"[5] to the president and his brother.

After returning from church, the president phoned former presidents Truman and Eisenhower, informing them that the crisis had indeed ended. He spoke with his brother at length and then, as Robert was leaving, the president said—in a reference to Abraham Lincoln's assassination shortly after his successful efforts to conclude the Civil War—"This is the night I should go to the theater." His brother replied, "If you go, I want to go with you."[6]

Khrushchev's conciliatory announcement stated that the Soviet Union would dismantle and remove their weapons from Cuba. ExComm members, including (*left to right*) Ted Sorenson, McGeorge Bundy, Robert Kennedy, and Kenneth O'Donnell, reconvened after receiving the message to clarify the terms of the agreement.

AMERICAN RESPONSE

The members of ExComm gathered for their tenth meeting in a far lighter mood than at any of the previous meetings. They stood up and applauded when the president entered the room, but he urged them to be careful, to avoid any public statements or attitudes that might humiliate or anger the Soviet leader. National Security Adviser McGeorge Bundy, who had favored the air strike option, noted, "Everyone knows who were the hawks [in favor of the air strike] and who were the doves [in favor of the blockade]. Today was the doves' day."[7] The group decided that there would be no air surveillance of Cuba that day, and that air surveillance beginning the next day would be carried out by the United Nations or other inspectors flying in a neutral plane.

President Kennedy later approved a formal response to Khrushchev's message, even though he had not yet received an official copy of the chairman's letter. "I am replying at once to your broadcast message of October twenty-eight," the response stated in part, "even though the official text has not yet reached me because of the great importance I attach to moving forward promptly to the settlement of the Cuban crisis. I think that you and I, with our heavy responsibilities for the maintenance of peace, were aware that developments were approaching a point where events could have become unmanageable. So I welcome this message and consider it an important contribution to peace. . . . I agree with you that we must devote urgent attention to the problem of disarmament, as it relates to the whole world and also to critical areas. Perhaps now, as we step back from danger, we can together make real progress in this vital field."[8]

Next, the president called the congressional leadership to the White House. Many who had only days earlier criticized his decision to institute the quarantine were now quick to congratulate him on the wisdom of his choice. "We've won a great victory," the president said. "We have resolved one of the great crises of mankind."[9]

The Soviet Union began almost immediately to dismantle the missile sites, even before President Kennedy had issued his response to Khrushchev's letter. The launching pads were destroyed with jackhammers. Missiles were loaded back onto ships headed for Russia.

The leader of Cuba, Fidel Castro, was furious at what he viewed as a betrayal by Khrushchev. "Cuba does not want to be a pawn on the world's chessboard. . . . I cannot agree with Khrushchev promising Kennedy to pull out his rockets without the slightest regard to the indispensable approval of the Cuban government,"[10] Castro stated.

Reports released more recently from Soviet archives show that Khrushchev had been deeply alarmed by the earlier letter from Castro urging him to make a preemptive nuclear strike against the United States, and that this in fact contributed to his ultimate decision to accept the terms offered by President Kennedy and remove the missiles from Cuba.[11] On October 30, he sent a private letter to Castro, explaining the reasons for his decision. "As we have learned from our ambassador," he wrote, "some Cubans have the opinion that the Cuban people want a declaration of another nature rather than the declaration of the withdrawal of the missiles. It's possible that this kind of feeling exists among the people. But we, political and government figures, are leaders of a people who doesn't know everything and can't readily comprehend all that we leaders must deal with. Therefore we should march at the head of the people and then the people will follow us and respect us. Had we, yielding to the sentiments prevailing among the people, allowed ourselves to become carried away by certain passionate sectors of the population and refused to come to a reasonable agreement with the U.S. government, then a war could have broken out, the course of which millions of people would have died and the survivors would have pinned the blame on the leaders for not having taken all the necessary measures to prevent the war of annihilation."[12]

A few days later, Soviet ambassador Dobrynin met with Robert Kennedy and attempted to hand him a letter in which Khrushchev sought to formalize the understanding involving the removal of American missile bases in Turkey. Robert Kennedy refused to accept the letter. The president would keep his promise, he assured the ambassador, but as noted earlier there could be no formal correspondence on the matter.

The president did keep his promise. The dismantling of the American missiles in Turkey began five months later, on April 1, 1963.

The 13 days in October had been a harrowing time for all involved—a time in which the United States had come closer than ever before to the brink of nuclear war. President Kennedy later gave a special gift to those who worked closely with him during the Cuban Missile Crisis. It was a silver calendar showing the month of October, with the 13 days of the crisis highlighted in a bold engraving.

LEGACY OF THE CUBAN MISSILE CRISIS

For 13 days in October 1962, the United States and the Soviet Union seemed to be on the brink of nuclear war. The slightest misunderstanding, a single unexpected event, or different decisions made by the leaders could have led to a catastrophic outcome.

Despite their differences, President John Kennedy and Chairman Nikita Khrushchev discovered that they had certain important things in common at that critical time. Both men had lived through a war and fought in the military; both knew how important it was that war be avoided. Both were determined to retain control of events, to listen to common sense and avoid the noise and distraction of those voices demanding a swift and harsh response to events.

Time was a key factor in the ability of the more moderate response to the crisis to be formed and enacted. For the first several days of the crisis, only a handful of Kennedy's close advisers knew of the discovery of the missiles in Cuba. This information was kept secret as the members of ExComm met, formulated possible responses, and gave the president their recommendations. President Kennedy, whose initial response was in support of an air strike, was able to step back and consider the advice and recommendations of several experts—some more moderate, others quite harsh—before reaching his own conclusions. It was only when the president had prepared and approved the U.S. response—the naval quarantine—that most Americans learned of the presence of the Soviet missiles

After Khrushchev's announcement, the Soviet missile sites in Cuba were destroyed immediately and most of the weapons were returned to the Soviet Union. Some of the disarmed missiles remain in Cuba as part of an exhibit in Havana (*above*).

in Cuba. Many, including Robert Kennedy, believe that if the ExComm discussions had been made public, or if there had been pressure to make a decision in a shorter period of time, the course taken by the United States would have been much different and far riskier.[13]

ExComm also provided a forum for debate and discussion, for disagreement, and for more debate. The members often met separately before meeting with the president, avoiding the tendency for group members to state only what they thought the president wanted to hear. The president sought the opinion of people from different departments, and so was exposed to many different views.

The memoirs of those involved in ExComm show that President Kennedy frequently attempted to view things from the Russian perspective, to understand how a particular action or consequence would be viewed by Chairman Khrushchev. Often, as Soviet records later showed, these efforts were unsuccessful. Yet, as Robert Kennedy noted in his memoirs, "Miscalculation and misunderstanding and escalation on one side bring a counterresponse. No action is taken against a powerful adversary in a vacuum. A government or people will fail to understand this only at their great peril. For that is how wars begin—wars that no one wants, no one intends, and no one wins."[14]

Both Kennedys believed that one of the lessons they had learned from the Cuban Missile Crisis was the importance of civilian control over the military. Many of the military leaders had urged a swift and immediate response to each event during the crisis; one—air force general Curtis LeMay—even expressed fury at the end, learning that Khrushchev had promised to dismantle the weapons. "It's the greatest defeat in our history," LeMay said. "We should invade today."[15] For Secretary of Defense Robert McNamara, who would later also serve under President Lyndon Johnson, the Cuban Missile Crisis led to an approach to foreign policy in which the United States would use a combination of toughness and restraint to coerce other nations into doing what they wanted.

This would prove a disastrous policy only a few years later in Vietnam. In 1965, the United States attempted to use American airpower as a demonstration of strength to the North Vietnamese Communists, using as a model the naval blockade of Cuba and how that had been a turning point in the Cuban Missile Crisis. The North Vietnamese did not respond as Khrushchev had; instead they matched each U.S. escalation with an escalation of their own. Clark Clifford, who succeeded McNamara as secretary of defense, noted that the architects of the Vietnam War were "deeply influenced by the lessons of the Cuban missile crisis. . . . Their successes in handling a nuclear showdown with Moscow had created a feeling that no nation as small and backward as North Vietnam could stand up to the power of the United States. They possessed a misplaced belief that American power could not be successfully challenged, no matter what the circumstances, anywhere in the world."[16]

Journalist Michael Dobbs suggests that the same mistaken lesson from the Cuban Missile Crisis occurred in the planning for the war in Iraq by President George W. Bush. In October 2002, shortly before the U.S. invasion of Iraq, President Bush quoted from President Kennedy's speech on October 22, 1962, saying that "we no longer live in a world where only the actual firing of nuclear weapons represents a sufficient challenge to a nation's security to constitute maximum peril."[17] The speech did not include the additional information that President Kennedy had, throughout the crisis, repeatedly been forced to resist pressure from his closest advisers to launch a military attack.

Some experts believe that the Cuban Missile Crisis triggered an acceleration in the arms race, as Soviet military officials rushed to acquire new weapons to ensure that the United States would not be in a position of strategic superiority. In particular, the Soviet leaders who followed Khrushchev greatly expanded their intercontinental ballistic missile program (missiles that could be launched at far greater distances) to match the U.S. missile program. The focus—on both sides—grew to preserve a sense of balance, to maintain an evenly matched arsenal (with each side hoping for a slight superiority) of nuclear weapons. There were few who believed, in the aftermath of the Cuban Missile Crisis, that a nuclear war would be "winnable" in the traditional sense; instead the focus shifted to ensuring that each side possessed sufficient nuclear weaponry to prevent the other side from attacking.

The lack of swift, effective ways for the leader of the Soviet Union and the leader of the United States to communicate directly had contributed to some of the misunderstandings and confusion that accelerated the crisis. A hotline was eventually developed to enable the two leaders to phone each other directly in the event of another crisis.

Kennedy adviser Ted Sorensen concluded his discussion of the Cuban Missile Crisis in his memoirs with the perhaps wishful statement that its successful resolution is the moment for which President Kennedy will be most remembered.[18] John Kennedy was assassinated in November 1963, a little more than a year after the crisis took place. His brother Robert was assassinated in California in June 1968 while campaigning to be elected president. Nikita Khrushchev was removed from office in October 1964, under charges that he had contributed to actions that damaged the prestige of his government and led the world to the brink of nuclear war. Cuban leader Fidel Castro remained in power until February 2008, when he was succeeded as Cuba's president by his brother Raúl. The United States does not currently have full diplomatic relations with Cuba, and travel by American citizens to the island is severely restricted and requires a special license.

CHRONOLOGY

1955 Nikita S. Khrushchev becomes leader of the Soviet Union.

1959 A revolution in Cuba, supported by the Soviet Union, brings Fidel Castro to power.

1960 John F. Kennedy is elected president of the United States.

1961 A wall is built separating eastern and western Berlin in August.

1962 **Late August** U.S. intelligence shows the Soviets engaging in major supply runs to Cuba.

September 4 Soviet ambassador Anatoly Dobrynin assures Attorney General Robert F. Kennedy that the Soviet Union is not transferring nuclear weapons to Cuba.

October 16 President Kennedy learns that nuclear missiles have been placed in Cuba. The president initially supports an air strike against the missile sites.

October 17 U-2 planes take photos revealing additional missile sites in Cuba.

October 18 Soviet foreign minister Andrei Gromyko assures President Kennedy that the Soviet Union has not placed offensive missiles in Cuba.

October 19 President Kennedy travels to Chicago; instructs advisers to reach a consensus on the U.S. response.

October 20 ExComm presents President Kennedy with two options: an air strike or a naval blockade.

October 21 President Kennedy decides to use a naval blockade first.

October 22 U.S. civilians are evacuated from U.S. military base in Cuba. President Kennedy addresses the nation, informing Americans of the existence of Soviet missiles in Cuba.

1962 ❧ **October 23** Aerial photos show that missiles are nearing a state of readiness. President Kennedy formally signs an order instituting the blockade, or "quarantine." Robert Kennedy meets with the Soviet ambassador and is again told that there are no offensive missiles in Cuba.

October 24 Soviet ships halt before reaching the quarantine boundary. In a letter to President Kennedy, Khrushchev accuses the United States of "outright banditry."

October 25 At the United Nations, U.S. ambassador Adlai Stevenson confronts Soviet representative

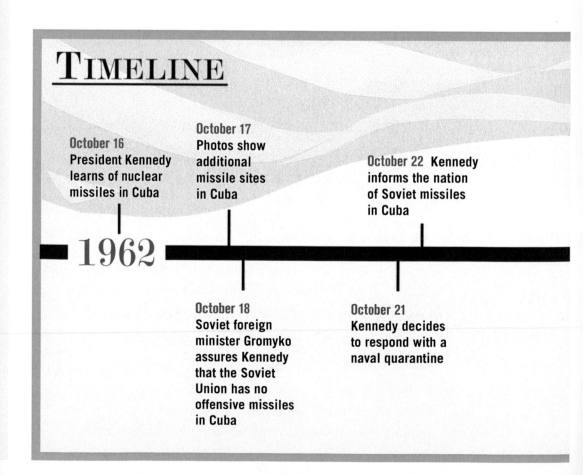

TIMELINE

October 16
President Kennedy learns of nuclear missiles in Cuba

October 17
Photos show additional missile sites in Cuba

October 22 Kennedy informs the nation of Soviet missiles in Cuba

1962

October 18
Soviet foreign minister Gromyko assures Kennedy that the Soviet Union has no offensive missiles in Cuba

October 21
Kennedy decides to respond with a naval quarantine

Valerian Zorin in the midst of his continued denials of the existence of the missiles; Stevenson presents photographic evidence demonstrating the presence of the weapons.

October 26 The first Soviet ship is stopped and inspected at the quarantine line. New photos show the existence in Cuba of Soviet short-range nuclear missiles that could be used against an invading force. President Kennedy orders the State Department to make plans for the establishment of a civil government in Cuba following an invasion; receives a letter from Khrushchev proposing a solution to the crisis.

October 24 Soviet ships halt before reaching the quarantine boundary

October 26 Kennedy receives a letter from Khrushchev proposing a solution to the crisis

October 28 Radio Moscow broadcasts a message from Khrushchev indicating that the missiles will be dismantled

1962

October 25 At the United Nations, U.S. ambassador Adlai Stevenson confronts Soviet ambassador Valerian Zorin

October 27 A second letter from Khrushchev is broadcast on Radio Moscow, demanding withdrawal of U.S. missiles from Turkey; An American U-2 pilot is shot down over Cuba

1962   **October 27** A second letter from Khrushchev is broadcast on Radio Moscow, demanding withdrawal of U.S. missiles from Turkey. An American U-2 pilot is shot down over Cuba; a second U-2 pilot strays into Soviet airspace. Castro urges Khrushchev to use nuclear missiles against the United States. President Kennedy decides to respond to Khrushchev's first letter; requests plans to be drawn up for an air strike.

October 28 Radio Moscow broadcasts a message from Khrushchev indicating that the missiles will be dismantled.

1963   Dismantling of U.S. missiles in Turkey begins on April 1. President Kennedy is assassinated in November.

1964   Khrushchev is removed from office in October.

NOTES

CHAPTER 1

1. Quoted in Michael Dobbs, *One Minute to Midnight: Kennedy, Khrushchev, and Castro on the Brink of Nuclear War*. New York: Alfred A. Knopf, 2008, p. 5.
2. Laurence Chang and Peter Kornbluh, eds., *The Cuban Missile Crisis, 1962: A National Security Archive Documents Reader*. New York: New Press, 1992, p. 3.
3. Transcript of the first Executive Committee Meeting, October 16, 1962, from the papers of John F. Kennedy, reprinted in Chang and Kornbluh, *The Cuban Missile Crisis, 1962*, p. 92.
4. Ibid., p. 94.
5. Quoted in Dobbs, *One Minute to Midnight*, p. 15.
6. Transcript of the second Executive Committee Meeting, October 16, 1962, from the papers of John F. Kennedy, reprinted in Chang and Kornbluh, *The Cuban Missile Crisis, 1962*, p. 101.
7. Ibid., p. 105.
8. Ibid., p. 112.
9. Ted Sorensen, *Counselor: A Life at the Edge of History*. New York: HarperCollins, 2008, p. 288.

CHAPTER 2

1. Thomas G. Paterson, *On Every Front: The Making of the Cold War*. New York: W.W. Norton, 1979, p. 8.
2. Ibid., pp. 14–15.

3. "The Construction of the Berlin Wall." Berlin International. http://www.berlin.de/mauer/geschichte/index.en.html.
4. Quoted in Dobbs, *One Minute to Midnight*, p. 34.
5. Quoted in Aleksandr Fursenko and Timothy Naftali, *Khrushchev's Cold War: The Inside Story of an American Adversary*. New York: W.W. Norton, 2006, p. 434.
6. Quoted in ibid., p. 454.
7. "Statement by President John F. Kennedy on Cuba, September 4, 1962." Mount Holyoke College. http://www.mtholyoke.edu/acad/intrel/jfkstate.htm.
8. Keith Eubank, *The Missile Crisis in Cuba*. Malabar, Fla.: Krieger, 2000, pp. 23–24.

CHAPTER 3

1. Robert F. Kennedy, *Thirteen Days: A Memoir of the Cuban Missile Crisis*. New York: W.W. Norton, 1969, p. 35.
2. Sorensen, *Counselor*, p. 288.
3. Ibid., p. 290.
4. Ibid., p. 39.
5. Ibid.
6. Sorensen, *Counselor*, p. 291.
7. Quoted in Michael R. Beschloss, *The Crisis Years: Kennedy and Khrushchev, 1960–1963*. New York: HarperCollins, 1991, p. 456.
8. Quoted in ibid.
9. Quoted in ibid., p. 457.
10. Kennedy, *Thirteen Days*, p. 43.

CHAPTER 4

1. Kennedy, *Thirteen Days*, p. 48.
2. Beschloss, *The Crisis Years*, p. 470.
3. Ibid.
4. Sorensen, *Counselor*, p. 296.
5. Quoted in Dobbs, *One Minute to Midnight*, p. 39.
6. Quoted in ibid.
7. Quoted in ibid., p. 42.
8. Quoted in Beschloss, *The Crisis Years*, pp. 481–482.
9. Sorensen, *Counselor*, p. 298.
10. Quoted in "John F. Kennedy: Address on the Cuban Crisis, October 22, 1962." Internet Modern History Sourcebook. http://www.fordham.edu/halsall/mod/1962kennedy-cuba.html.
11. Quoted in ibid.
12. Quoted in ibid.
13. Sorensen, *Counselor*, p. 300.
14. Beschloss, *The Crisis Years*, p. 485.
15. Dobbs, *One Minute to Midnight*, p. 50.
16. Kennedy, *Thirteen Days*, p. 57.
17. Ibid, p. 58.
18. Quoted in Dobbs, *One Minute to Midnight*, p. 73.

CHAPTER 5

1. Kennedy, *Thirteen Days*, pp. 69, 71.
2. Quoted in Dobbs, *One Minute to Midnight*, p. 88.
3. Ibid., p. 91.
4. "Letter from Chairman Khrushchev to President Kennedy, October 24, 1962." Mount Holyoke College. http://www.mtholyoke.edu/acad/intrel/nikita.htm.
5. Quoted in Dobbs, *One Minute to Midnight*, p. 131.
6. Ibid., p. 138.

7. Kennedy, *Thirteen Days*, p. 83.
8. Ibid., p. 85.

CHAPTER 6

1. Quoted in Beschloss, *The Crisis Years*, p. 521.
2. "Telegram from the Embassy in the Soviet Union to the Department of State, October 26, 1962, 7 P.M." Kennedy-Khrushchev Exchanges, U.S. Department of State. http://www.state.gov/www/about_state/history/volume_vi/exchanges.html.
3. Kennedy, *Thirteen Days*, p. 93.
4. "Message from Chairman Khrushchev to President Kennedy (the Second Letter), October 27, 1962." Mount Holyoke College. http://www.mtholyoke.edu/acad/intrel/nikita3.htm.
5. Kennedy, *Thirteen Days*, p. 94.
6. Quoted in Beschloss, *The Crisis Years*, p. 527.
7. Kennedy, *Thirteen Days*, p. 96.
8. Ibid., p. 97.

CHAPTER 7

1. "Prime Minister Fidel Castro's Letter to Premier Khrushchev, October 26, 1962." National Security Archive, George Washington University. http://www.gwu.edu/~nsarchiv/nsa/cuba_mis_cri/docs.htm.
2. Quoted in Beschloss, *The Crisis Years*, p. 535.
3. Quoted in Dobbs, *One Minute to Midnight*, p. 306.
4. Quoted in ibid., pp. 308–309.
5. "Memorandum for the Secretary of State from the Attorney General, on Robert Kennedy's

October 27 Meeting with Dobrynin." National Security Archive, George Washington University. http://www.gwu.edu/~nsarchiv/nsa/cuba_mis_cri/docs.htm.

6. "USSR, Cable, Top Secret, Dobrynin Report of Meeting with Robert Kennedy on Worsening Threat, October 27, 1962." National Security Archive, George Washington University. http://www.gwu.edu/~nsarchiv/nsa/cuba_mis_cri/docs.htm.

7. Dobbs, *One Minute to Midnight*, p. 310.

CHAPTER 8

1. "Letter from Chairman Khrushchev to President Kennedy, October 28, 1962."

2. Quoted in Beschloss, *The Crisis Years*, p. 541.

3. Quoted in ibid., p. 542.

4. Sorensen, *Counselor*, p. 305.

5. Kennedy, *Thirteen Days*, p. 110.

6. Ibid.

7. Quoted in "Summary Record of the Tenth Meeting of the Executive Committee of the National Security Council, October 28, 1962." John F. Kennedy Presidential Library and Museum. http://www.jfklibrary.org/cmc.

8. "Department of State Telegram Conveying President Kennedy's Reply to Chairman Khrushchev, October 28, 1962." John F. Kennedy Presidential Library and Museum. http://www.jfklibrary.org/cmc.

9. Quoted in Beschloss, *The Crisis Years*, p. 545.

10. Quoted in ibid., p. 550.

11. Dobbs, *One Minute to Midnight*, p. 321.

12. "USSR, Letter, from Chairman Khrushchev to Prime Minister Castro, October 30, 1962." National Security Archive, George Washington University. http://www.gwu.edu/~nsarchiv/nsa/cuba_mis_cri/docs.htm.

13. Kennedy, *Thirteen Days*, p. 111.

14. Ibid., p. 125.

15. Quoted in Dobbs, *One Minute to Midnight*, p. 335.

16. Quoted in ibid., p. 347.

17. Quoted in ibid., pp. 347–348.

18. Sorensen, *Counselor*, p. 309.

BIBLIOGRAPHY

Beschloss, Michael R. *The Crisis Years: Kennedy and Khrushchev, 1960–1963*. New York: HarperCollins, 1991.

Bialer, Seweryn, and Michael Mandelbaum. *The Global Rivals*. New York: Alfred A. Knopf, 1988.

Blight, James G., and David A. Welch. *On the Brink: Americans and Soviets Reexamine the Cuban Missile Crisis*. New York: Hill and Wang, 1989.

Brugioni, Dino A. *Eyeball to Eyeball: The Inside Story of the Cuban Missile Crisis*. New York: Random House, 1991.

Chang, Laurence, and Peter Kornbluh, eds. *The Cuban Missile Crisis, 1962: A National Security Archive Documents Reader*. New York: New Press, 1992.

Dobbs, Michael. *One Minute to Midnight: Kennedy, Khrushchev, and Castro on the Brink of Nuclear War*. New York: Alfred A. Knopf, 2008.

Eubank, Keith. *The Missile Crisis in Cuba*. Malabar, Fla.: Krieger, 2000.

Fensch, Thomas, ed. *The Kennedy-Khrushchev Letters*. The Woodlands, Tex.: New Century Books, 2001.

Fursenko, Aleksandr, and Timothy Naftali. *Khrushchev's Cold War: The Inside Story of an American Adversary*. New York: W.W. Norton, 2006.

Gribkov, Anatoli I., and William Y. Smith. *Operation ANADYR: U.S. and Soviet Generals Recount the Cuban Missile Crisis*. Chicago: Edition Q, 1994.

Kennedy, Robert F. *Thirteen Days: A Memoir of the Cuban Missile Crisis*. New York: W.W. Norton, 1969.

Morgan, Patrick M., and Keith L. Nelson, eds. *Re-viewing the Cold War: Domestic Factors and Foreign Policy in the East-West Confrontation*. Westport, Conn.: Praeger, 2000.

Paterson, Thomas G. *On Every Front: The Making of the Cold War*. New York: W.W. Norton, 1979.

Sorensen, Ted. *Counselor: A Life at the Edge of History*. New York: HarperCollins, 2008.

WEB SITES

American President: John Fitzgerald Kennedy

http://millercenter.org/president/kennedy

Berlin International: The Berlin Wall

http://www.berlin.de/mauer/index.en.html

The Cuban Missile Crisis, 1962: The Documents

http://www.gwu.edu/~nsarchiv/nsa/cuba_mis_cri/docs.htm

Eleanor Roosevelt National Historic Site: Nikita Khrushchev (1894–1971)

http://www.nps.gov/archive/elro/glossary/khrushchev-nikita
.htm

Harry S. Truman Library and Museum

http://www.trumanlibrary.org

Internet Modern History Sourcebook: John F. Kennedy; Address on the Cuban Crisis, October 22, 1962

http://www.fordham.edu/halsall/mod/1962kennedy-cuba.html

John F. Kennedy Presidential Library and Museum

http://www.jfklibrary.org

Mount Holyoke College: Letter from Chairman Khrushchev to President Kennedy, October 24, 1962

http://www.mtholyoke.edu/acad/intrel/nikita.htm

Mount Holyoke College: Statement by President John F. Kennedy on Cuba, September 4, 1962

http://www.mtholyoke.edu/acad/intrel/jfkstate.htm

Public Broadcasting Service: Nikita Khrushchev (1894–1971)

http://www.pbs.org/redfiles/bios/all_bio_nikita_khrushchev.htm

Robert F. Kennedy Center for Justice and Human Rights

http://www.rfkmemorial.org

U.S. Department of State: Kennedy-Khrushchev Exchanges

http://www.state.gov/www/about_state/history/volume_vi/exchanges.html

The White House

http://www.whitehouse.gov

FURTHER READING

Chang, Laurence, and Peter Kornbluh, eds. *The Cuban Missile Crisis, 1962: A National Security Archive Documents Reader.* New York: New Press, 1999.

Dobbs, Michael. *One Minute to Midnight: Kennedy, Khrushchev, and Castro on the Brink of Nuclear War.* New York: Alfred A. Knopf, 2008.

Kennedy, Robert. *Thirteen Days: A Memoir of the Cuban Missile Crisis.* New York: W.W. Norton, 1999.

May, Ernest R., and Philip D. Zelikow, eds. *The Kennedy Tapes: Inside the White House During the Cuban Missile Crisis.* New York: W.W. Norton, 2002.

Munton, Don, and David A. Welch. *The Cuban Missile Crisis: A Concise History.* New York: Oxford University Press, 2006.

Stern, Sheldon. *The Week the World Stood Still: Inside the Secret Cuban Missile Crisis.* Stanford, Calif.: Stanford University Press, 2004.

WEB SITES

Avalon Project: The Cuban Missile Crisis

http://avalon.law.yale.edu/subject_menus/msc_cubamenu.asp

Yale University's online archive contains 275 documents related to the Cuban Missile Crisis, including summaries of ExComm meetings and confidential memos, letters, and transcripts of telephone conversations.

The Berlin Wall

www.newseum.org/berlinwall

An interactive exhibit that details the history and politics behind the Berlin Wall, how the news differed in East and West Berlin, and the impact of Soviet rule.

The Cuban Missile Crisis 1962: The 40th Anniversary

www.gwu.edu/~nsarchiv/nsa/cuba_mis_cri

The National Security Archive at George Washington University provides declassified documents, audio clips, photographs, and analysis.

Exploration of Kennedy's Presidency

http://www.pbs.org/wgbh/amex/presidents/35_kennedy/index .html

PBS's interactive site offers biographical materials, an opportunity to vote on the "hot issues" in the election of 1960, and primary source material (including letters and speeches) from the Cuban Missile Crisis.

PHOTO CREDITS

PAGE

3: ©Pictorial Press Ltd/Alamy

7: AP Images

15: AP Images

17: ©ITAR-TASS Photo Agency/ Alamy

27: AP Images

31: AP Images

39: AP Images

43: AP Images

47: ©Popperfoto/Getty Images

51: ©Peter Newark American Pictures/The Bridgeman Art Library

54: AP Images

61: AP Images

70: ©Gamma-Keystone/Getty Images

74: ©Time & Life Pictures/Getty Images

76: ©Getty Images

82: ©Archive Photos/Getty Images

87: ©Chris Hammond/Alamy

INDEX

A

Acheson, Dean, 26, 28, 38–39
air strikes. *See* military air
  strikes option
air surveillance of Cuba. *See*
  photographs and air surveillance of Cuba
alliances, 11–12
allies, warnings to, 6, 38–39
Anderson, Rudolf, Jr., 71
arms race, 89

B

Ball, George, 4, 9
Bay of Pigs Invasion, 16
Berlin blockade and air lifts,
  14
Berlin Wall, 2, 14–16
Beschloss, Michael, 37, 45
blockade of Berlin, 14
blockade (quarantine) of Cuba
  discussed as option, 6, 25,
    26–27, 33, 36
  ExComm review of, 50
  first ship boarded, 55–57
  first Soviet ships approaching,
    50–52
  formal proclamation of, 48
  Kennedy's announcement of,
    44
Boggs, Hale, 38
Bucharest (Soviet ship), 55
Bundy, McGeorge, 1, 4, 79, 82, 83
bunkers, underground, 76–77
Bush, George W., 89
Bush, Prescott, 24

C

cabinet of the president, 38
Carter, Marshall, 8

Castro, Fidel
  Cuban Revolution and, 2
  fate of, 90
  Khrushchev's letter to, 85
  possibility of negotiation
    with, 8
  proposed letters to, 25
  responses to Khrushchev, 73,
    84–85
Central Intelligence Agency
  (CIA), 1, 4, 8, 35
Churchill, Winston, 13
civilian control of military, 88
Clifford, Clark, 88
Cold War, 2, 11–12
communication delays, 60–61,
  89–90. *See also* letters
congressional leaders, 38, 39–40,
  77, 84
Cuba
  decision to place missiles in,
    20
  defensive weapons in, 2–4
  Gromyko on, 30–32
  invasion possibility, 7, 9,
    58–59, 71, 78
  See also Castro, Fidel; *specific
    topics*
Cuban Revolution, 2

D

de Gaulle, Charles, 38–39
Dillon, Douglas, 4
Dobbs, Michael, 89
Dobrynin, Anatoly
  letter delivered to, 74–75
  meetings with Robert Ken-
    nedy, 20, 32, 48–49, 74–76,
    82, 85
  meeting with Dean Rusk, 42

E

Eastern Europe and Western
  Europe, 13
Eisenhower, Dwight D., 1–2, 19,
  82
elections, U.S., 19
Europe, division of, 13
ExComm (Executive Commit-
  tee of the National Security
  Council)
    final meeting, 83–84
    as forum for debate and dis-
      cussion, 87–88
    Kennedy's gift to members of,
      86
    Khrushchev, things in com-
      mon with, 86
    Khrushchev letters, discussion
      of, 65, 69–71
    Khrushchev radio broadcast
      and, 79, 82
    meeting after decision, 46
    meetings on options, 4–10,
      22–25, 25–27
    preparations for possible
      attack, 77–78
    quarantine review by, 50
    recommendations by, 28–30,
      35–37
    secrecy and, 86–87
    State Department meetings,
      32–33

F

France, 38–39
Free Rocket Over Ground
  (FROG) missiles, 58

G

Germany, divided, 2, 14
Great Powers era, 12–13
Gromyko, Andrei, 30–32
Guantanamo Bay Naval Base,
  Cuba, 38, 45

H

Hoover, J. Edgar, 65

I

intercontinental ballistic missiles,
  89
intermediate-range ballistic missiles, 2, 43
invasion of Cuba
    as option, 7, 9, 71
    plans for, 58–59, 78
Iraq War, 89
iron curtain, 13
Italy, missiles in, 2, 53

J

Johnson, Lyndon, 53
Joint Chiefs of Staff, 28, 35, 71
Joseph P. Kennedy, Jr. (U.S.
  destroyer), 55

K

Kefauver, Estes, 19
Kennedy, Caroline, 5
Kennedy, Ethel Skakel, 23
Kennedy, Jacqueline Bouvier, 18
Kennedy, John F.
    assassination of, 19, 90
    background of, 16
    Bay of Pigs Invasion and, 16
    decision of, 37–38
    ExComm meetings and,
      4–10, 22, 28, 35–37
    initial reaction, 1
    invasion plans order by,
      58–59
    letters from Khrushchev, 52,
      60–65, 66–71
    letters to Khrushchev, 40–41,
      72–76
    past, awareness of, 11
    profile of, 18–19
    Profiles in Courage, 18–19
    public address, 42–45

Russian perspective sought by, 88
secrecy, difficulty of, 34–35
statements by, 21, 32
Stevenson and, 53
Why England Slept, 18
Kennedy, Joseph, 18
Kennedy, Joseph, Jr., 18
Kennedy, Patrick, 18
Kennedy, Robert
   assassination of, 90
   on counterresponses, 88
   Dobrynin meetings, 20, 32, 48–49, 74–76, 82, 85
   draft letter, 73
   ExComm and, 7, 9, 22–24, 35, 46
   Hoover letter to, 65
   naval blockade and, 28–29
   profile of, 23
   on quarantine, 51
   on seriousness of situation, 58
   Soviet war preparations and, 68–69
   Thirteen Days, 24
   UN and, 53
Khrushchev, Nikita
   background, 16–17, 20
   Castro's letter to, 73
   decision to place missiles, 20
   ExComm discussions about, 9
   Kennedy, things in common with, 86
   Kennedy's letters to, 40–41, 72–76
   letters from, 52, 60–65, 66–71, 85
   profile of, 56–57
   proposed letters to, 25, 28–30
   Radio Moscow statement, 79–82
   removal from office, 90
Kimovsk (Soviet ship), 50

L
LeMay, Curtis, 28, 88
letters
   from Castro to Khrushchev, 73
   from Hoover to R. Kennedy, 65
   Kennedy's responses to Khrushchev, 72–76, 84
   Kennedy's "will and determination" letter to Khrushchev (Oct. 22), 40–41
   to Khrushchev and Castro, proposed, 25, 28–29
   Khrushchev's Oct. 24 letter, 52
   Khrushchev's Oct. 26 letter, 60–65
   Khrushchev's Oct. 27 letter, 66–71
   Khrushchev's Oct. 28 radio broadcast, 79–82
   Khrushchev to Castro, 85
   refused letter on Turkey missiles, 85
   Sorensen asked to draft a warning letter, 29–30
Lundahl, Arthur, 4–5

M
Marucla (Soviet ship), 55–57
McCarthy, Joseph, 23
McCone, John, 4
McNamara, Robert
   ExComm and, 4
   on invasion option, 58
   lessons from the Crisis, 88
   missile sites progress report and, 69
   naval blockade and, 26, 28, 48
medium-range ballistic missiles, 21, 42–43
military, importance of civilian control over, 88

military air strikes option
    after Khrushchev's letters, 71
    consideration of, 6, 25–26, 28,
        36–37
    nuclear war as probably out-
        come of, 37–38
    war plans, 78
military superiority, U.S., 17
missile erectors, 47

N
National Photographic Interpre-
    tation Center, 57
National Security Council, 35.
    See also ExComm
NATO (North Atlantic Treaty
    Organization), 2. *See also*
    Turkey, NATO missiles in
naval blockade. *See* blockade
    (quarantine) of Cuba
Nixon, Richard, 19
nuclear war
    air strikes option and, 37–38
    Khrushchev on, 65
    the past and, 11
    planning for the worst, 76–78
    possibility of, 10, 24, 34, 48
    potential damage from, 40–41
    as "winnable," 89

O
Oswald, Lee Harvey, 19

P
past, role of, 11–13
photographs and air surveillance
    of Cuba
    first evidence, 4–5, 8
    low-flying set showing more
        detail, 46–47
    second set of photos, 22, 28
    Soviet troops and FROG
        missiles shown by, 57–58

suspension of, 84
    U-2 plane shot down, 71, 75
    UN meeting and, 55
power vacuum, 13
Profiles in Courage (Kennedy),
    18–19
public address by Kennedy, 42–45
public address by Khrushchev,
    79–82
public opinion, 29

Q
quarantine of Cuba. *See* blockade
    (quarantine) of Cuba

R
Radio Moscow address, 79–82
retaliation from Soviet Union,
    possibility of, 8–9
Ribicoff, Abraham, 24
Rusk, Dean, 6, 8, 42, 52, 65

S
Salinger, Pierre, 35
secrecy, 34–35, 86–87
Sorensen, Ted
    on air strikes, 37
    draft letter, 73
    ExComm and, 4, 9–10
    on ExComm debates, 25
    on legacy of the Crisis, 90
    speeches prepared by, 33, 45
    warning letter attempted by,
        29–30
Soviet Union
    Berlin Wall and, 14
    Cold War and, 11
    Cuban Revolution and, 2
    defensive weapons placed in
        Cuba, 2–4
    intercontinental ballistic
        missiles, 89
    lessons from the Crisis, 89

possible responses of, 8–10,
  35–36
ships from, 50–52, 55–57
transport of missiles to Cuba,
  21
at UN, 53–55
war preparations by, 68–69
*See also specific topics and
  persons*
space program, U.S., 19
spy planes. *See* photographs and
  air surveillance of Cuba
Stalin, Joseph, 17, 56–57
State Department, U.S., 32–33
Stevenson, Adlai, 19, 53–55
Strategic Air Command, 9
Sweeney, Walter, 36–37

T
Taylor, Maxwell, 4
telegrams, 64
television broadcast of UN Security Council meeting, 52–55
Thirteen Days (R. Kennedy), 24
Thompson, Llewellyn, 4
time as key factor, 86–87
Truman, Harry, 82
Turkey, NATO missiles in
  dismantling of, 85
  installation of, 2
  in Khrushchev's letter, 66–68,
    69–70
  military superiority and, 17
  as negotiating tool, 53
  possible reciprocal action
    against, 26, 27, 70
  refused letter on, 85

scheduled for withdrawal,
  75–76

U
U-2 spy plane flights over Cuba.
  See photographs and air sur-
  veillance of Cuba
U-2 spy plane in Soviet airspace,
  72
underground bunkers in West
  Virginia, 76–77
United Nations Security Coun-
  cil, 45, 52–55, 67
United States. *See specific topics
  and people*

V
Vietnam War, 19, 88–89

W
war preparations, 68–69, 76–78
Western Europe and Eastern
  Europe, 13
West Virginia underground
  bunkers, 76–77
Why England Slept (Kennedy),
  18
"will and determination" letter,
  40–41
World War II, 12

Y
Yuri Gagarin (Soviet ship), 50

Z
"zones of influence," 13
Zorin, Valerian, 53–55

About the Author

HEATHER LEHR WAGNER is a writer and editor. She is the author of more than 40 books that explore political and social issues and focus on the lives of prominent men and women, including several books on the presidency and presidential elections. She has also written *The Watergate Scandal* for the MILESTONES IN AMERICAN HISTORY series.

Wagner earned a B.A. in political science from Duke University and an M.A. in government from the College of William and Mary. She lives with her family in Pennsylvania.